TOP FUEL DRAGSTER

1963 onwards (all models)

Dedicated to

Andy Welberry – my Dad, my friend (my love of drag racing is all your fault!) – and my family, who give me so much joy every day.

First published in October 2014

A catalogue record for this book is available from the British Library

ISBN 978 0 85733 265 3

Library of Congress control no: 2013935231

Published by Haynes Publishing,
Sparkford, Yeovil,
Somerset, BA22 7JJ, UK.
Tel: 01963 442030
Fax: 01963 440001
Int. tel: +44 1963 442030
Int. fax: +44 1963 440001
E-mail: sales@haynes.co.uk
Website: www.haynes.co.uk

Haynes North America Inc.,
861 Lawrence Drive, Newbury Park,
California 91320, USA.

Printed in the USA by Odcombe Press LP,
1299 Bridgestone Parkway, La Vergne, TN 37086.

TOP FUEL DRAGSTER

1963 onwards (all models)

Owners' Workshop Manual

An insight into the technology, engineering and maintenance of an 8,000bhp, 300+mph, 6G accelerating, 0–100mph in less than one second Top Fuel dragster

Dan Welberry

Contents

OPPOSITE Andy Carter launches the Lucas Oil Top Fuel dragster at Santa Pod Raceway in front of a packed spectator bank. In the time it took to read the previous sentence he covered a ¼ mile! *(Dom Romney)*

RIGHT Concentration ahead of a run. Driving a Top Fuel dragster requires the driver to be completely focused. *(Gary Cottingham)*

Introduction

Top Fuel dragsters are the quickest and fastest racing cars on the planet. In justification of this statement I simply invite you to read the stunning statistics given in the following sidebar.

TOP FUEL DRAGSTER PERFORMANCE STATISTICS

- Acceleration from 0 to 100mph in under a second.
- Start-line G pulled is around 6G – twice that experienced by a space shuttle crew on take-off.
- Power output around 8,000bhp.
- One Top Fuel dragster's 500cu in Hemi produces more horsepower than the first eight rows at the NASCAR Daytona 500.
- Under full throttle, a dragster engine consumes 1.5 gallons of nitro per second, the same rate of fuel consumption as a fully loaded 747 but with four times the energy volume.
- The supercharger takes more power to drive than a stock Hemi engine makes.
- Dual magnetos apply 44A to each spark plug. This is the output of an arc welder in each cylinder.
- Within three seconds, the car will be travelling at over 260mph. By the time it has reached the quarter-mile race distance it will be travelling at over 330mph.
- A Top Fuel dragster can cover a quarter of a mile in 4.4 seconds.
- If all the equipment is paid off, the crew has worked for free and *nothing blows up*, each run costs $2,000 per second.

(Some of the above information is used by kind permission of www.wdifl.com.)

I'm hoping that I now have your full attention, as we prepare to unpack these awesome machines in great detail, and try to dispel some of the myths that surround drag racing. For many people drag racing isn't a respectable form of motorsport, and the fact that they don't 'do' corners makes it simply pointless. Quotes similar to 'Anyone can drive fast in a straight line' usually accompany such negativity. So in this book we'll look at what makes this statement laughable when the drivers' ability and the technology required to achieve such incredible performances are taken into consideration.

So what is drag racing? Put simply, drag racing is a side-by-side race in a straight line over a quarter-mile distance, for both cars and motorbikes. A drag race will take place at a purpose-built facility or a track that's been established on an old airfield with a long enough runway. Although the cars may race over a quarter mile, the quicker cars then need another half mile to slow down again. There are two lanes on a drag strip, as each race is between only two vehicles.

The early pioneers of the sport would be waved off down the track by a flag, but these days a series of lights known as a Christmas Tree, located in the centre of the track at the start, trigger the commencement of the race. At the start line there are three beams of light across the lane. When a vehicle's front wheels break the first beam it's deemed to be in 'pre-stage', and at the very top of the Christmas Tree a bulb will illuminate. When the second beam – or 'stage beam' – some 6–8in further

ahead is broken it triggers a second Christmas Tree light just below the first, letting the driver or rider and their opponent know that they're ready to race, as they're on the start line.

Below the pre-stage and stage bulbs are three much larger amber bulbs. For a number of classes, these will light one after the other at five-tenths of a second intervals ahead of another five-tenths of a second to the green light. However, classes such as Top Fuel use what's known as a 'pro-tree', which is where all three amber lights come on simultaneously, with a four-tenths of a second gap before the green light.

I mentioned earlier that there was a third beam. This sits slightly beyond the start line, and if broken before the green light comes on will trigger a 'red light', the red bulb at the foot of the tree. No racer wants to see this, as it means a false start and immediate elimination from the competition.

A further beam sits 60ft out from the start line and provides the first recorded time point. This is where it gets impressive for a Top Fuel dragster – because it'll be at that 60ft mark

> *'Alcohol is for drinking, gas is for cleaning parts, and nitro is for racing!'*
>
> **Original author unknown**

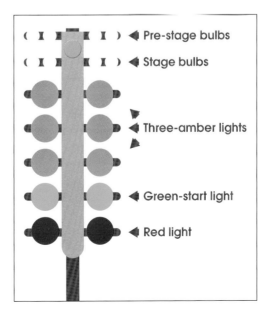

Pre-stage bulbs
Stage bulbs
Three-amber lights
Green-start light
Red light

ABOVE Top Fuel dragsters are the quickest and fastest racing cars on the planet. Here four-time FIA European Top Fuel champion Andy Carter burns out at Santa Pod Raceway. Andy's previous car, owned by Andersen Racing, as well as his former crew chief and crew members, have been instrumental in putting this book together. *(Dom Romney)*

(Illustration by 3tc)

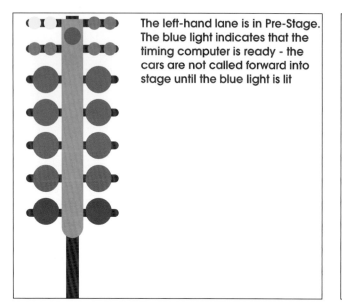

The left-hand lane is in Pre-Stage. The blue light indicates that the timing computer is ready - the cars are not called forward into stage until the blue light is lit

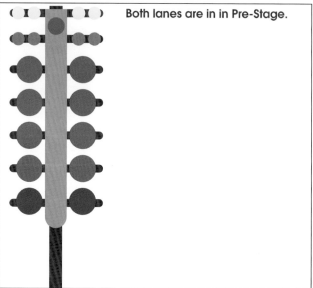

Both lanes are in in Pre-Stage.

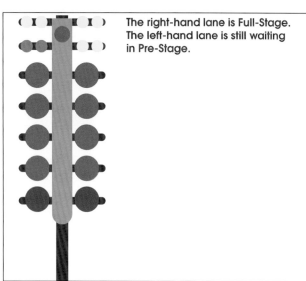

The right-hand lane is Full-Stage. The left-hand lane is still waiting in Pre-Stage.

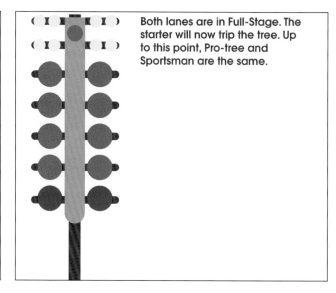

Both lanes are in Full-Stage. The starter will now trip the tree. Up to this point, Pro-tree and Sportsman are the same.

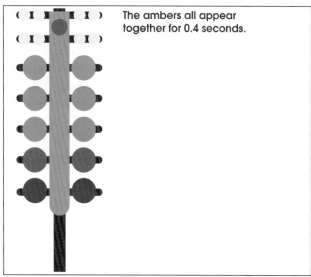

The ambers all appear together for 0.4 seconds.

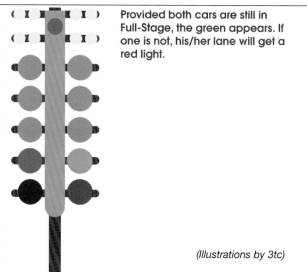

Provided both cars are still in Full-Stage, the green appears. If one is not, his/her lane will get a red light.

(Illustrations by 3tc)

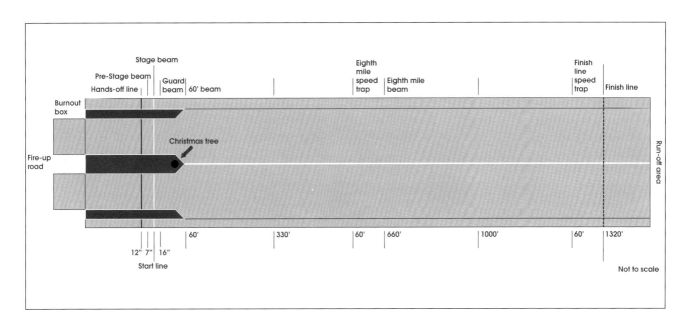

(Illustration by 3tc)

in around 0.8 of a second and will already be doing a speed of 100mph! A further beam is positioned at the 330ft mark, which a Top Fuel dragster will break in around two seconds, and another beam at the halfway point will be broken in around three seconds, when the car will be travelling at around 280mph. The final two beams, or 'traps' as they're known, are at the finish line – one measuring speed and the other recording the time taken to cover the quarter mile, known as the elapsed time or 'ET'. A Top Fuel dragster will stop the traps at 4.4 seconds and will be travelling at over 330mph.

Although the traditional quarter-mile distance (ie 1,320ft) is currently run by every other class of dragster, the distance raced by both Top Fuel dragsters and Fuel Funny Cars was reduced after the death of American Funny Car pilot Scott Kalitta in 2008. Following this tragedy the National Hot Rod Association (NHRA) introduced a 1,000ft distance as a theoretically temporary measure while safety measures were reviewed. However, to this day this lesser distance remains in place in the USA, and now also in Australia (the ANDRA) and Europe, with the FIA European Top Fuel championship changing its rules accordingly in 2012. Top Fuel cars cover this new distance in 3.7 seconds at around 330mph.

You'll read in the following chapter a more in-depth outline of the history of the Top Fuel dragster; but aside from the stunning stats presented, what is this incredible class of

vehicle, and where does it sit alongside the other classes in this straight-line sport?

'Top Fuel' is the pinnacle class in drag racing for both cars and bikes. For the purpose of this book we'll focus on the cars where 'Sportsman ET' is the entry level. This class is open to cars running 12-second ETs or lower. An ET or elapsed time is the time taken for the vehicle to cover the quarter-mile race distance.

From here the sport is made up of various classes running head-to-head with no time restrictions, or running to an 'Index', eg not quicker than 10.90 seconds (Super Street), not quicker that 9.90 seconds (Super Gas) or not quicker than 8.90 seconds (Super Comp). Anyone running quicker than the class limit

BELOW The various car classes in drag racing: Sportsman ET is the entry level. This class is open to cars running 12-second ETs or slower.
(Mark Skinner)

RIGHT Super Street – an 'Index' class for cars running slower than 10.90 seconds. Anyone running quicker than the class limit 'breaks out', and eliminates themselves in racing eliminations or forfeits the run in qualifying.
(Mark Skinner)

'breaks out' and eliminates themselves in racing eliminations or forfeits the run in qualifying.

There are also classes where cars that can cover a quarter mile as quick as 6.0 seconds can race a car that covers it in 8.99 seconds and anything in between. To make these races fair, each racer will 'dial in' their expected times, and the difference between these times will be used as the handicap on the Christmas Tree starting lights. Simply put, the car running to the six-second dial-in will be delayed at the start by two seconds if they're racing a car with an eight-second dial-in. In theory they should both be crossing the finish line at around the same time, making for a close race; but if either runs quicker than their dial-in, then they eliminate themselves. This can seem confusing, but it makes for some great racing. The 'heads up' classes, with no time restrictions, also add to the great mix within the sport of drag racing.

BELOW Super Gas – for cars not quicker than 9.90 seconds.
(Mark Skinner)

As well as various other rules affecting class regulations, *eg* engine size, another distinguishing factor is the fuel used. This includes everything from regular pump petroleum and specifically manufactured race fuels right up to the ultimate fuel – nitromethane. It's the use of nitro that gives the ultimate class its name: Top Fuel.

One of the appeals of drag racing is the incredible diversity of vehicles on display at any race meeting. Some will be based on modern or current vehicles from Europe or the US, while others tend to lean towards more classic cars, such as my personal favourites the 1957 Chevrolet Bel Air or the 1967 Ford Mustang. Other varieties might include more 'hot rod'-style classics, such as the Ford Popular.

Of course, these cars – despite being classic – all have doors, whereas a variety of classes are contested by other vehicles that look less conventional, such as an 'Altered' or the more traditional 'dragster'. For most people the characteristic image of a dragster will be a long, thin design with smaller front wheels, large rear wheels and a wing on the back, and the Top Fuel dragster is the ultimate extreme of this image, with the longest allowed wheelbase, the highest and largest rear wing, and the ultimate in construction of rear wheels to handle the

massive power output from one of the largest permitted engine configurations.

As well as the competition classes, drag racing also offers a high degree of 'show' at any event, with exhibition vehicles such as rocket- and jet-powered cars and bikes and vehicles known as 'Wheelstanders' that can cover the entire quarter mile on their rear wheels!

In the various chapters of this book you'll read about the Top Fuel dragster in great

ABOVE Super Comp – for cars not quicker than 8.90 seconds. *(Mark Skinner)*

LEFT A variety of classes are contested by vehicles that look less conventional than a standard-looking car with doors, such as an 'Altered'. Here the Havoc Fuel Altered performs a flame burnout. *(Mark Skinner)*

depth, including information on the history and evolution of the class, the design and construction of the cars, their maintenance away from and at the track during a race weekend and, of course, the incredible experience of what it's like to drive one of these machines. These accounts have been provided by some of the best-known names in European Top Fuel racing and give great insight into the required procedures prior to and after a run up the track, as well as the experience of what it's like to be propelled over a quarter of a mile in less than five seconds at 300mph.

So how did this book come about? I'm a long-time drag racing fan and I've attended races since I was ten years of age. My father was first exposed to drag racing at the British International Drag Festival on 19 September 1964, held at Blackbushe Airport, and having been hooked by the sport he was keen to share it with me. So I was taken drag racing even prior to my tenth birthday, but I didn't really get it. I mean, it was colourful, loud and seemed pretty cool, but each race was over so quickly, and I guess I just missed the point.

Not wishing to give up, my father took me to Blackbushe once more, and this time something seemed to click. I was still struggling to see any point in the lower classes that we know today as the 'Sportsman' classes, but the sight and sound of a Top Fuel dragster or Funny Car doing a burnout and then making

a full pass had me captivated. It's not just the sight, it's the complete assault on the senses, including the smell of burning rubber and nitro, the incredible vibration that you feel through your whole body as the ground shakes, as well as the awesome visual treat. So forget fishing – from then on my dad and I could be found at either Long Marston Raceway (now Shakespeare County Raceway) or Santa Pod Raceway at weekends. Those weekends have given me the best memories of my childhood.

As my career developed in design and marketing I used this as my way into the sport. At the Santa Pod Raceway Main Event in 2001 I approached Top Fuel driver Andy Carter to offer my services in marketing, PR and sponsorship procurement duties. I went on to become his longest-serving crew member, with ten years of service to the team.

Andy Carter announced his retirement from racing in 2011 following a hugely successful time in FIA Top Fuel dragster competition, having won four FIA Top Fuel Dragster championships. The curtain finally came down on his record-breaking career at the Santa Pod Raceway European Finals in September of that year.

A result of this decision is that it's allowed me to tap into his knowledge and experience for the purposes of this Haynes manual, without the constant backdrop of racing pressures. It's also meant that the strong relationship with the

Andersen Racing Top Fuel team established during Andy's racing career has enabled us to use their dragster as a feature car for the majority of the shots in this book. This is the same car that took Andy to two of his FIA European Top Fuel titles, in 2008 and 2009.

I'm so grateful to Andy, who's driven from his Greater London home to my offices on the south coast whenever required, as well as having invited me to his home, despite his busy schedule with his son and current karting star Albert. The input from Andy has been a huge help, as has his network of contacts. Being able to pick up the phone and ask questions of some of the most knowledgeable names in European racing, such as Andy Robinson, Jon Webster and Ben Allum, has been invaluable. Simply put, I couldn't have written this book without Andy.

As my experience is very much on the marketing side, I'll try to make this book as accessible as possible to enthusiasts whilst at the same time providing the real meat from a technical perspective. Insight from some of the biggest names in Top Fuel drag racing, both in Europe and 'Big Daddy' Don Garlits from the USA, will also provide an unprecedented insight into the ultimate motorsport vehicle – the Top Fuel dragster.

Dan Welberry
June, 2014

ABOVE 'Funny Cars' are the nitro-burning cousins of the Top Fuel dragster, with a much shorter 125in wheelbase, full body and the driver sitting behind the 500in³ motor. *(Mark Skinner)*

Acknowledgements

I owe a huge debt of gratitude to everyone associated with this book. I've been amazed at the willingness of so many people, who've dropped everything to supply me with information and images so swiftly. It's a real testament to the drag racing community, and I really appreciate it.

My special thanks go to: Andy Carter – for technical input and interviews; Per and Karsten Andersen for allowing the use of their entire operation for photographic reference; Ben Allum for technical input; 'Big Daddy' Don Garlits and Darryl Bradford for interviews and imagery; Kim Reymond, Rico Antes and Shelley Pearson for interviews; Don Ewald for text provision and imagery (www.wdifl.com); Brian Taylor for historical advice; Mark Skinner for feature car and additional photography; Tog (Andy Rogers) for additional imagery (www.eurodragster.com); Julian Hunt for additional imagery (www.julianhunt.net); Gary Cottingham for additional imagery; and Gary Page, Sarah Senderski and Gareth Robinson for interviews.

Chapter One

The Top Fuel dragster story

The early 1950s dragsters were the product of a curious mix of experimentation. The media often referred to them as 'rail jobs', because their creators would remove the body and pretty much everything else from the donor vehicle other than the engine and seat, and mount it on to frame rails.

OPPOSITE The early dragsters: Car No 25 – built and raced by Art Chrisman – raced at the first NHRA Nationals in 1955, and is photographed here at the Goodwood Festival of Speed 2008. *(Dan Welberry)*

During this period some incredible creations were witnessed, including single front-engined vehicles, single rear-engined, dual engine combinations, and three- and even four-engined cars. These might be positioned either one behind the other or side-by-side on the track, and some were even four-wheel drive. As far as engine manufacturers went, pretty much every make was tried and tested at some point, including Chevrolet, Pontiac, Chrysler, Buick, Cadillac, Lincoln, GMC, Oldsmobile and even aircraft engines.

Some racers opted for no body at all in an effort to save weight. Others would use partial bodies, and yet others created their own bodies to achieve some sort of aerodynamic shape. It really was a case of 'let's try it and see if it works!'

This period of evolution eventually saw most of the early racers opt for a front engine combination with the driver positioned right at the back of the car, sitting over the differential. Purpose-built chassis started to appear soon afterwards, and dragsters began to transform into what we'd now call a 'slingshot', 'rail' or 'digger'.

LEFT Barnstormer, lovingly recreated by Ron Johnson. Originally driven by Tommy Ivo in 1962, it is seen here at the Goodwood Festival of Speed 2008.
(Dan Welberry)

Parallel with the development of the cars, the sport itself underwent something of an evolutionary process. Long before the first British International Drag Festival at Blackbushe Airport in the mid-'60s, drag racing had established itself as a hugely popular form of motorsport in America. The Salt Flats of Bonneville saw drag racers running against the clock as early as the late '40s, but it wasn't until the early '50s that the first dedicated drag strip was established – Santa Ana drag strip at Orange County Airport, California. In 1951

America's NHRA (National Hot Rod Association) was founded, and it held its first official race in 1953 on the LA County Fairground car park. After some $6 million investment over the years, the same facility remains in use to this day and is now known as Pomona Raceway.

These early days saw very rapid development in dragster technology as well as speed, and by 1959 parachutes had become mandatory for cars exceeding 150mph. In 1963 Top Fuel was introduced as a professional class and the flag-waving starter was replaced

BELOW Beebe and Mulligan Fuel Dragster, recreation of the 1969 Winternationals winning car of 1969. Photographed at the Goodwood Festival of Speed 2008.
(Dan Welberry)

1965: Maynard Rupp becomes the first Top Fuel champion.

1965–73: The Top Fuel champion is determined by the winner of the World Finals race rather than a season-long championship.

1966: John Mulligan records the first six-second quarter-mile run.

1971: Don Garlits campaigns the first rear-engined dragster following a serious accident in his front-engined car caused severe damage to his right foot.

1972: 'TV' Tommy Ivo records a 5.97 elapsed time (ET). It was so much quicker than anyone else that the figure was regarded as being somehow incorrect, and wasn't recognised! A month later Mike Snively ran a 5.97 at 235.69mph to record the sport's first official five-second run.

1973: Shirley Muldowney becomes the first female to gain a Top Fuel dragster licence.

1975: Don Garlits wins his first NHRA Top Fuel title. He would go on to win two more in 1985 and 1986.

1977: Shirley Muldowney becomes the first female Top Fuel champion.

1980: Shirley Muldowney becomes first repeat Top Fuel champion.

1988: Eddie Hill runs first four-second pass, earning the nickname 'The Four Father'.

1992: Kenny Bernstein achieves first 300mph run.

1999: Tony Schumacher runs an incredible 330mph.

2008: The death of Funny Car racer Scott Kalitta causes the NHRA to review race distances and the decision is made for Top Fuel/ Funny Car races to be run over 1,000ft rather than the full 1,320ft (quarter mile).

2008: Tony Schumacher becomes the all-time NHRA Top Fuel total wins leader, overtaking Joe Amato.

2004–09: Tony Schumacher dominates the Top Fuel class with six straight titles, his seventh title overall.

To date, Tony Schumacher holds the record for the quickest and fastest Top Fuel runs over a quarter mile: ET 4.428 seconds, speed: 336.15mph.

At the time of writing Brown holds the ET record over 1,000ft – 3.701 seconds. Spencer Massey is the fastest, though, 332.18mph.

In FIA European competition, Andy Carter holds the quarter-mile ET record at 4.572 seconds, with Risto Poutiainen the speed record-holder at 317.06mph. The European record ET and speed record over the 1,000ft distance are currently held by Thomas Nataas: 3.965 at 306.99mph.

by the Christmas Tree of starting lights. Soon after the introduction of Top Fuel, class legend Don Garlits ran the first 200mph speed over a quarter mile in 1964.

By this time pioneer racers such as Garlits, Tommy Ivo and Tony Nancy were all making a name for themselves in the sport, and it wasn't long before the NHRA sent these and other racers to Europe to promote the sport. The adjacent sidebar highlights key Top Fuel milestones over the years in the USA.

The following text has been provided by the hugely popular drag racing website 'We Did It For Love' (www.WDIFL.com). The first piece, from Stan Weber, helps to illustrate the rate of development that made Top Fuel drag racing so dangerous, meaning that something had to be done to make the sport safer. The second article, from Don Ewald, provides his own views, and an eyewitness account, of the event that changed the face of Top Fuel for ever. I'm really grateful to them for allowing me to use these pieces in this book, as I believe they really help to illustrate this significant chapter in the history of the class:

From front- to rear-engine dragsters
by Stan Weber (used by kind permission of www.wdifl.com)

'By the end of the '60s, horsepower gains had once again passed tyre and clutch technology. The traction advantage gained years earlier, by locating the driver behind the rear tires (in the traditional "slingshot" layout) was no longer enough to assure adequate bite. In addition, top end speeds over 220mph were the order of the day. As a result of tyre growth at high speed, the fuelers were finding their rear tyres attached to the track by only the narrowest of "footprints" (the amount of tyre actually in contact with the track surface) – a situation that forebode certain disaster.

'Their gracefully pointed frames, suspensions, and exposed steering components distorted grotesquely at speed. Something needed to be done that would enhance start-line traction and improve stability and control. In addition, the newfound horsepower – and its resulting stress on engine and driveline components – was taking a heavy toll on driver wellbeing.

'Sitting just three feet behind a motor that's producing a dozen times its original horsepower had never been particularly safe. But as these pioneers continued to gain more and more power from their old hemis, goggle-coating "oil baths" were becoming so common that many drivers began taping rags to the back of their driving gloves in the hope of being somewhat prepared for the inevitable. Engine and supercharger failures became increasingly violent, and the word "explosion" was becoming an all-too-familiar adjective when describing engine breakage.

'Perhaps the worst of the dangers (at least in frequency of occurrence), was engine fire. Scores of '60s slingshot drivers experienced painful and sometimes disfiguring burns to their hands and faces (and indeed, some even lost their lives) when fuel – or a mixture of fuel and oil – ignited and blew back on them. Yet, even in light of those events – and with all its obvious faults – in 1969 the venerable slingshot was still firmly implanted as king of the dragsters.

'There were a number of attempts to develop a viable rear-engine design, but despite a few moderate successes, something "big" was needed to force an across-the-board move away from the slingshots, and sure enough, the driver who had earned that very nickname was soon to deliver.

'On March 8, 1970, dragster legend Don Garlits experienced a horrific transmission explosion on the starting line at Lions drag strip. This time, fire was not the main problem. His car's slingshot configuration had dictated that his legs and feet straddle the two-speed transmission. When it blew apart, with all the force of a military land mine, shrapnel tore off the front half of his right foot.

'While still in his hospital bed, Garlits swore to himself that this was to be the last run that he would make in a slingshot dragster, and began to formulate a design that would, once and for all, put the fuel motor – and all of its terrible potential – behind him.

'After taking time to evaluate the weaknesses of past rear-engine cars, Garlits and Connie Swingle put their fertile minds to work. While stories vary as to just who was responsible for the final breakthrough, the gist of it was to

LEFT Don Garlits is a 3-time NHRA Top Fuel champion and one of the classes true innovators. *(Don Garlits Collection)*

BELOW Don Garlits waits for his turn to race prior to the run that would change the Top Fuel class for ever. *(Don Ewald)*

substantially slow the steering ratio. This "trick" helped negate the driver's tendency to over-respond when correcting for rear-end movement (either real or imagined – without the entire car in front for visual reference, some drivers found the forward cockpit location disorienting).

'With a few test runs under his belt, Big Daddy headed West. After a successful tune-up session at Lions, Garlits pulled into the pits at the 1971 NHRA Winternationals towing a small, sleek car that was deceptively simple – almost underwhelming in appearance – except for the fact that its motor was placed between the driver and the rear wheels.

'Once on the tarmac, though, the little car quickly got everyone's attention!

'During the meet, Garlits marched unmercifully through the top fuel field, enjoying a wide performance margin – and all the while, making it look as easy and casual as taking the family out for a Sunday afternoon cruise. The die had been cast. The performance potential of the rear-engine layout had been painfully driven home to the sport's premiere drivers, builders, and sponsors. And now that the handling issue had obviously been sorted out, there would be no turning back. Immediately following that race, the chequebooks came out, and there was a rush to the chassis shops.

'Virtually every top chassis builder was faced with an overwhelming demand to produce a rear-engine design of his own. There were some unique variants, to be sure, but for the most part chassis lengths remained about the same and the initial batch of "modern-day" rear-engine cars retained the traditional look – almost as though sections of the chassis had simply been rearranged.

'In hardly any time at all, rear-mounted wings appeared and took a permanent place above the rear tires. As further experimentation caused the rear-engine/rear-wing concept to become ever more effective, the cars began to grow in size and length, evolving into the graceless behemoths we see in Top Fuel today.

'The slingshots are forever gone from the big league Top Fuel wars, but their spirit – and many of the drivers who loved them – lived on during a period of transition throughout the early to late '70s.'

The day that changed the face of drag racing

by Don Ewald (used by kind permission of www.wdifl.com)

'On March 8, 1970, amid a cool Winter night in Long Beach, California, the face of drag racing changed forever. It was the AHRA (American Hot Rod Association) Grand American – their first big race of the year. The stands of Lions drag strip were still full of the 25,000+ fans who'd stayed on to to see the Top Fuel final between "Big Daddy" Don Garlits and the infamous Richard Tharp in the Creitz & Donovan fueler. After their burnouts both cars staged without any games. Starter Larry Sutton flipped the switch and in an instant Tharp red-lighted (left the start line ahead of the green starting light) and Garlits headed into history.

'Garlits was running an overdrive B&J two-speed transmission with some of his own designs. When he hit the throttle it was like a bomb went off. The two-speed literally blew up and the results were immediate and devastating. The car was cut in half, severing Garlits' right foot at the arch in the process. Pieces went everywhere including the stands. One spectator lost an arm and another suffered near fatal injuries. I was standing right behind the car, and believe me, it was something I'll never forget. While recuperating, Don made up his mind to design a front-driver car that would be competitive in the 1970s and history will bear out that he did.

BELOW On 8 March 1970 dragster legend Don Garlits experienced a horrific transmission explosion on the starting line at Lions drag strip. His car's slingshot configuration had dictated that his legs and feet straddle the two-speed transmission. When it blew apart, with all the force of a military land mine, shrapnel tore off the front half of his right foot. *(Don Garlits private collection)*

LEFT The car splits in two with Garlits still strapped between the rear wheels. *(Don Ewald)*

CENTRE As the car comes to rest, the safety crew are quickly on the scene to attend to Garlits. *(Don Ewald)*

BOTTOM LEFT With the car now in two sections, the front half of the chassis containing the motor is left sideways across the track. The damage provides some idea of the force of the explosion. *(Don Ewald)*

BOTTOM RIGHT When he hit the throttle it was like a bomb went off. The two-speed literally blew up and the results were immediate and devastating. The car was cut in half, severing Garlits' right foot at the arch in the process. *(Don Fwald)*

'The early rear-engine dragsters were shaky at best. In parallel to the quantum leaps Top Fuel took in 1962 and 1963, so was the evolution of the front-driver cars in 1971–1973. In the beginning we basically took the entire combination out of our rear-driver cars and plugged them into a new chassis. Some barbarians actually cut up their front-engine dragsters and converted them to rear-engine. None of those were successful.

'We soon found out that the same things that worked in the front-engine cars would not work with the rear-engine cars. As we learned the unique characteristics of the new design (ie steering ratio changes and rear end changes) the cars got more stable and easier to drive. We also had to go through some very painful lessons that this breed of dragster brought with them – a new set of safety issues. Kenny Logan and Bob Edwards both paid dearly to show that the single and double element Armco barriers so common then were too high from the track to the bottom rail. Herm Petersen is a painful reminder that we needed better firesuits, not lighter ones. Marvin Schwartz gave his all to illustrate that more stringent chassis specs were called for.

'Nonetheless, even with these exceptions, the fatality rate dropped drastically in the dragster ranks and Garlits' dream of a safer car was realised. However, for many of us these new cars were at first a challenge and then a bore. Speaking for myself, they were not nearly as much fun to drive as the front-engine cars. Even when we started going much quicker and much faster, they were for the most part – boring. I guarantee that's not the perspective you'll get from someone who never drove a front-engine dragster!'

European Top Fuel

There is, I believe, no definitive first British Top Fuel car. Brian Taylor – author of the Haynes title *Crazy Horses* – knows his history and tells me that there's a rumour that the Mk I Allard Chrysler Dragster did have a small percentage of nitro added. The Mk II car was launched in 1965 as a methanol burner but may well have had fire added to the pipes when driven by Alan Allard or Clive Skilton. The Allard name may well be familiar to many through the famed Allard car company and its founder, Sydney Allard. Sydney was involved in many forms of motorsport including drag racing, where he was something of a pioneer. His son

LEFT 'We are going to build one of these!' These were the words of Sydney Allard as he stormed into his office one day in 1960, slamming a copy of *Hot Rod Magazine* on the table. He had spotted a feature on American Chris Karamesines' latest Chizler rail, and it was this that spawned the birth of Britain's first dragster – the Allard Chrysler that now resides at the National Motor Museum, Beaulieu. (www.theaccelerationarchive.co.uk/acag/acag.html) *(Bob Roberts)*

ABOVE **Commuter dragster – one of the UK's best-looking slingshot dragsters ever.** *(Mark Skinner)*

Alan was also actively involved in the family's motorsport activity as a driver, and was one of the co-founders of the British Drag Racing Association (BDRA) in 1963. Clive Skilton began his drag racing career in 1967, when he won the Street Eliminator class before taking over the driving duties of the Allard Dragster in 1968.

An early car that really looked the part was the Commuter dragster. Again, this car was run on methanol but may have had nitro mixed in for good measure at some point or other.

Unveiled in 1968, the Tudor Rose was another dragster that really looked and sounded the business. It was a collaboration between UK drag racing pioneer Rex Slugget and future Top Fuel legend Dennis Priddle. Whilst Dennis set about drawing up plans for the long-wheelbase car, Rex headed to the States to purchase the best Keith Black drivetrain components he could find, the Keith Black Hemi having rapidly become the engine of choice for Top Fuel racers. (Keith Black's name has been synonymous with drag racing for decades. A one-time seller of parts, he went on to race boats before his development and production of the aluminium Chrysler Hemi engine block that became the industry standard. Between 1975 and 1984 all the national records in Top Fuel drag racing were set by dragsters using Keith Black blocks. In 1995 Keith was inducted into the Motorsports Hall of Fame of America along with the likes of Bruce McLaren.)

This was a major turning point in the development of a proper Top Fuel dragster in Europe, and the Tudor Rose's early shakedown runs looked promising. During its first outings at the 1968 Easter meeting at Santa Pod it was covering the quarter mile in the ten-second bracket before dropping well into the nines at over 160mph. By July of that year it had broken the 180mph barrier, and by the end of the year had achieved a best of 182mph, dipping well into the low eights. However, this was to be the end of the project, as funds had actually prevented the car from running on nitro, and everything they'd achieved had been done running methanol.

Around this time the Allard/Skilton dragster was running nitro, but as stated previously, there really is no 'first' European Top Fuel dragster.

By the early 1970s, Top Fuel slingshots (front-engined dragsters) were up to speed in the UK, with two names very much at the forefront of the class: Dennis Priddle and Clive Skilton. In 1971 Skilton became the first British driver to break the 200mph barrier with a strong 7.39 ET at 203mph. It was Priddle, however, who would claim the honour as the first European racer into the six-second bracket, with a 6.99 ET at 185mph in 1972. The two would go on exchanging blows in the early '70s, with both heading to the States in 1973 where they became the first UK drag racers to enter an American event. Following an engine explosion Skilton had switched to rear-engined dragsters, whilst Priddle remained in the front-engined configuration (see 'From front- to rear-

FUNNY CARS

Funny Cars are the second tier class in drag racing behind Top Fuel. Whereas Top Fuel cars follow the traditional 'dragster' design, Funny Cars at least look something like roadgoing cars, with carbon fibre bodies based loosely on a production vehicle. That's about as close as it gets, though. Underneath the flip-up body is a purpose-built racing car with the same amount of power under the right foot as the Top Fuel cars. They have a wheelbase of 125in, and the driver – much like the original slingshot dragsters – sits behind the motor, over the differential. The term 'Funny' comes from the experimental years of the class in the 1960s: the early pioneers would move the rear wheels forward, adjusting the wheelbase and improving weight transfer under acceleration as well as providing better traction. It was at this point in their evolution that they earned the tag 'Funny Cars'. The modern Funny Car can cover the 1,000ft distance in 3.9 seconds at around 320mph.

BELOW '**Funny Cars**' **look something like a road-going car with a carbon fibre body based loosely on a production vehicle – in this case a Saab (or a Dodge Stratus).** (Mark Skinner)

engine dragsters' on page 18). By 1974 two new names had entered the Top Fuel ranks: Roz Prior and Peter Crane. Roz became the first female Top Fuel dragster pilot outside of the USA, and would go on to become a serious competitor.

In Easter 1976 history was made with the first eight-car 'Pro Fuel' field. An estimated

record 50,000 crowd packed Santa Pod Raceway to witness the spectacular race, which included such names as US legend 'Big Daddy' Don Garlits, Clive Skilton, Owen Hayward, Allan Herridge and Peter Crane. In round one Crane found himself up against Garlits, and to the delight of the monster crowd not only took the win but, even more importantly, recorded the first five-second run in Europe at 5.97 seconds.

Even Radio One DJ Dave Lee Travis became a Top Fuel pilot, with a very respectable 6.66 ET at 220mph best. However, despite the popularity of the Top Fuel dragsters, Funny Cars soon took over as the favourite 'fuel' (nitro-burning) class, with the 1980 Santa Pod World Finals seeing 20 Funny Cars entered, including racers from both the USA and Europe.

By the mid-'80s UK Top Fuel legend Dennis Priddle had retired from the sport to concentrate on building cars and parts, and with the ranks of the Funny Cars continuing to grow the Top Fuel class began to suffer.

The Top Fuel tide finally started to turn in the late '80s, when team owner Rune Fjeld imported an ex-Joe Amato car from the States to be driven by Liv Berstad. At this time Pelle

Lindelow and Monica Oberg were recording Europe's first Top Fuel side-by-side five-second run at Pitea drag strip in Sweden, and the four Top Fuel entries in the 1988 World Finals at Santa Pod soon afterwards were all Scandinavian.

Top Fuel saw out the '80s on a high, with American Top Fuel star Darrell Gwynn invited to Santa Pod in 1989, where he and Liv Berstad recorded the UK's first side-by-side fives.

The '90s dawned with the return of Darrell Gwynn at the Santa Pod Easter meeting. This meeting saw Gwynn suffer a terrible accident where he hit the barrier at around three-quarters of the way through his pass. He remained in a UK hospital for many weeks before returning to the USA. Sadly he was left paralysed, as well as losing the lower part of his left arm. The accident left the UK drag racing scene in complete shock.

At this time there were a number of cars in Europe but organisation was required to take the pinnacle class forward, by making it more attractive to sponsors and promoters. Keith Bartlett formed the European Top Fuel Association, creating the European Top Fuel Challenge. The first race of this new series in

1991 saw eight cars entered. Top Fuel was on the way back!

New names appeared throughout the early '90s, and in 1995 one man stepped up from a successful period in the Outlaw Anglia class – Andy Carter.

Bartlett continued his heavy involvement with the sport, purchasing Santa Pod Raceway in 1996, the same year that the new FIA European Drag Racing championship was contested. This was a major development for drag racing in Europe, as the FIA cachet brought real credibility to the pro classes and their championships.

Another name coming up through the ranks during this period was England's Barry Sheavills, moving up from Pro Comp dragster (now Top Methanol dragster). Barry was one of three racers invited by Rico Anthes to join him at the Hockenheim NitrolympX for a four-car demo exhibition, along with Kent Persson and Pelle Lindelow. It was here that Europe would see its first ever four-second ET, with Persson recording an amazing 4.99 ET at 293mph. Barry went on to record the UK's first four-second run in 1998 at Santa Pod Raceway – 4.97 at 297mph. He also went on to take the FIA European Top Fuel championship that year.

FAR LEFT US Top Fuel star Darrell Gwynn suffered a terrible accident when he hit the barrier at around three-quarters of the way through his pass at Santa Pod Raceway.
(Gary Cottingham)

LEFT Andy Carter stepped up to Top Fuel following a successful period in the Outlaw Anglia class.
(Andy Carter Collection)

ABOVE Andy Carter versus Barry Sheavills – Europe's first 300mph runs, Europe's first side-by-side four-second pass, and Carter's 4.89 was the quickest outside of America. Barry Sheavills 4.97 ET at 304mph; Andy Carter 4.89 ET at 303mph. *(Andy Carter Collection)*

In the early 2000s the Top Fuel class included many names who would go on to play a huge part in dragster history for years to come. Anita Makela, Micke Kågered, Kim Reymond, Barry Sheavills and Andy Carter were all making a name for themselves, but it is perhaps the FIA Main Event of 2002 that most race fans will remember with greatest fondness. Andy and Barry were paired together in qualifying, and somehow you just knew that something big was about to happen. They went on to record Europe's first 300mph runs and first side-by-side four-second pass, and Carter's 4.89 was the quickest outside of America. There was also a new FIA European ET record: Barry Sheavills 4.97 ET at 304mph; Andy Carter 4.89 ET at 303mph.

Throughout the decade the Top Fuel class continued to stay strong, with the Fuel Funny Car class being the one to struggle. Fuel FC was not an FIA championship class, so many nitro racers opted for Top Fuel instead. During this time Carter claimed four FIA European Top Fuel titles, including back-to-back championships in '08 and '09. Urs Erbacher currently has three titles to his name following his own back-to-back successes in 2010–11.

A full list of FIA European Top Fuel champions and NHRA Top Fuel champions can be found in the Appendices.

Needless to say, many other names have also played a significant part in the history of European Top Fuel history. For a full history of European drag racing, see *Crazy Horses* by Brian Taylor (ISBN 978 1 84425 425 5).

USA leads the way

Unlike Europe, Top Fuel has remained a strong class throughout in the US, with many of the sport's superstars contesting the NHRA series. Don Garlits is a name you'll no doubt be accepting by now as one of the true legends of drag racing, but he's just one of many who've made their mark in Top Fuel history. Soon after Garlits had introduced his rear-engine design in '71, 1972 saw the first Top Fuel car into the five-second ET bracket, driven by Tommy Ivo. He was so much quicker than anyone else that it was thought to be a timing error and was therefore not recognised. Mike Snively went on to post a 5.97 ET a month later, making his the name that 'officially' sits alongside this huge milestone.

In 1973 the name of Shirley Muldowney appeared in the Top Fuel entry list as the first woman to contest the class. In 1977 she would claim her first championship, before doing the same again in 1980, making her the first ever repeat NHRA Top Fuel champion.

The world would have to wait until 1988 to see the first ever four-second run in the class. Eddie Hill earned himself a new nickname off the back of that achievement – 'The Four Father'.

As well as incredible elapsed times in the Top Fuel class, speeds were on the increase, with Kenny Bernstein the first to reach 300mph in 1992 at the Texas Motoplex, Dallas. Believe it or not, by 1999 a man by the name of Tony Schumacher had set a new mark of 330mph, and the world wondered just how much quicker could these cars really go? Schumacher went on to claim his first Top Fuel title in the same year.

Now, I don't know if there's something in the name, but Schumacher would go on to win *seven* NHRA Top Fuel titles, with six of them coming consecutively from 2004–09.

As mentioned in the Introduction, probably the most significant event in the class' history was the change from its traditional quarter-mile distance to 1,000ft. As is explained there, this was originally bought in as a temporary safety measure to reduce top-end speeds following the death of US Funny Car racer Scott Kalitta. His car had failed to slow in the 'shutdown' area at the end of the quarter mile following a huge engine explosion around the finish, in which his parachutes were damaged. He had consequently continued at speed and was killed following a high-speed impact.

To this day the 1,000ft distance remains in place for all NHRA and FIA European Top Fuel competition, yet despite this measure speeds continue to remain incredibly high, with the 1,000ft speed record a staggering 332.18mph at the time of writing, recorded by Spencer Massey – just 4mph slower than the quarter-mile record. 2012 NHRA Top Fuel champion Antron Brown holds the ET record at 3.701.

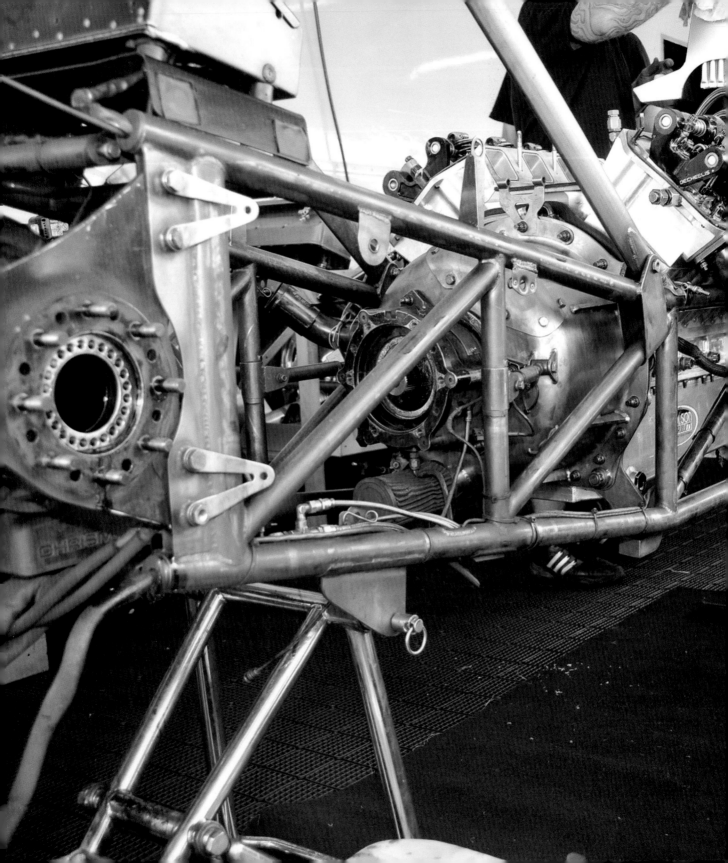

Chapter Two

The anatomy of the Top Fuel dragster

The Top Fuel dragster is a superb piece of engineering – from its chassis, through to the nitro-burning, 8,000bhp engine. In this chapter we'll look at the design, construction and evolution of a Top Fuel dragster, as well as its safety features.

OPPOSITE The engine dominates the chassis. The engine is mounted solidly at the front, via a T6 grade aluminium engine mount that's bolted to brackets on the chassis. *(Mark Skinner)*

Chassis

The most distinctive feature of a Top Fuel dragster is its overall length. This hasn't always been the case, and reference has already been made in the history section to the early front-engined dragsters. However, as the sport evolved to rear-engined designs and speeds increased, the overall length has stretched to that of the virtual missiles we see today.

During the early years the overall wheelbase was much shorter than current designs. The '60s front-engine dragsters started life at a very modest 100in, but it was soon apparent that more length was required to improve traction and keep the front wheels on the ground, pushing the driver further back behind the motor.

Over time the front-engine dragster would evolve to an overall wheelbase in excess of 200in, while chassis builders also experimented with the engine position. Length peaked at 220in, which was utilised for the first successful rear-engine dragster, designed and built by Don Garlits – Swamp Rat 14.

The front-engined 'slingshot' cars were becoming increasingly dangerous as they struggled to handle the increasing speeds and heightened the risk of fire erupting directly in front of the driver. The new rear-engine design would provide better traction, more stability,

greater strength and, most importantly, with the engine behind the pilot would provide better driver safety.

The development of the rear-engined chassis design is arguably the single most important development in the Top Fuel dragster's history. Swamp Rat 14 was to become the blueprint for modern designs, and the overall stance of today's cars remains very similar.

The modern chassis

The biggest difference between the pioneering '70s car and the modern Top Fuel dragster remains their overall wheelbase. Current rules state that this mustn't exceed 300in nor be less than 280in, with most teams opting for the optimum length that seems to perform best.

The chassis on a Top Fuel dragster is the central structure to which everything else is attached. It's built from 4130 chromoly steel tubing, and all tubes and brackets are tig-welded. 4130 steel is a collection of steel grades specified by the Society of Automotive Engineers (SAE). They have an excellent strength-to-weight ratio and are considerably stronger and harder than other standard steels. The '41' denotes a low alloy steel containing around 1% chromium and 0.2% molybdenum, these materials often being referred to as chromoly steel. The '30' denotes the carbon content. The full breakdown of 4130 chromoly steel is:

Carbon	0.28–0.33%
Chromium	0.8–1.1%
Manganese	0.7–0.9%
Molybdenum	0.15–0.25%
Phosphorus	0.035% max
Silicon	0.15–0.35%
Sulphur	0.04% max

The chassis must be able to handle the considerable stresses that go hand-in-hand with 5–6G acceleration at launch and the negative 6G under deceleration, as well as protecting the driver from any angle in the event of an accident and allowing a degree of flex – a chassis can curve upwards as much as 8in between the axles on a run. It must not be plated or painted after construction.

When static, the minimum ground clearance

ABOVE The front section housing the fuel cell, main fuel line, steering rack and timing systems for the fuel and clutch. *(Mark Skinner)*

must be 3in from the front of the car to 12in behind the centreline of the front axle and 2in for the remainder of the car other than the oil pan.

Essentially the Top Fuel chassis is made up of three sections. The front section houses the fuel cell, main fuel line, steering rack and the timing systems for the fuel. The front wheels are attached to a titanium spindle by one central nut. This spindle is attached to an upper and lower A-arm that's then welded or bolted to the top and bottom chassis rails.

BELOW The front wheels are attached to a titanium spindle by one central nut. This spindle is attached to an upper and lower A-arm that's then welded or bolted to the top and bottom chassis rails.

(Mark Skinner)

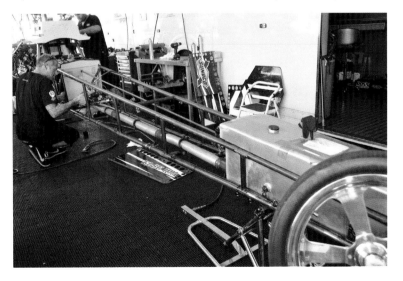

ABOVE **The centre section contains the driver's compartment complete with roll cage, which connects to the chassis at six points.** *(Gary Cottingham)*

ABOVE **The rear section houses the engine, clutch, direct drive, reverser and axle. The engine is mounted solidly at the front, via a T6 grade aluminium engine mount that's bolted to brackets on the chassis.** *(Mark Skinner)*

ABOVE AND BELOW **Both the driver's section and the rear have additional tubing between the top and bottom rails positioned at angles. This creates triangular sections that provide additional strength where it's required the most.** *(Mark Skinner)*

The centre section contains the driver's compartment complete with roll cage, which connects to the chassis at six points.

Finally, the rear section houses the engine, clutch, direct drive, reverser and axle. The engine is mounted solidly at the front, via a T6 grade aluminium engine mount that's bolted to brackets on the chassis. The rear motor plate is made of ¼in chromoly and is sandwiched between the rear of the engine block and the clutch titanium bellhousing. The rear motor plate is then bolted to brackets on the top and bottom chassis rails.

Both the driver's section and the rear have additional tubing between the top and bottom rails positioned at angles. This creates triangular sections offering additional strength where it's required the most. The chassis is designed and built in a way that allows the front and rear sections to break away from the central driver's section in the event of a crash.

The driver's cockpit tubing is made of a larger diameter tube with a thicker wall. The front and rear section tubing can then slide into the larger tubing, as their diameter and wall thickness are smaller. These smaller tubes are then welded at the point where they pass into the cockpit tube, naturally creating a weaker breaking point.

The driver's seat is made of carbon fibre and is attached to the chassis by Dzus fasteners. These fasteners locate to brackets that are tig-welded to the chassis rails for fixing in place.

Each chassis must be tested and passed by SFI before it's permitted for use. SFI, in their words, 'administer standards for speciality/performance automotive and racing equipment'. They were originally a foundation run by SEMA (the Speciality Equipment Market Association), so the initials 'SFI' stood for SEMA Foundation Inc', and although the SFI is now independent from SEMA the name remains. The chassis must pass SFI inspection not only on first building but also during every year thereafter, to make sure that it conforms to current specification updates.

Design and manufacture

Unlike teams in Formula 1, European Top Fuel drag racing teams operate on small budgets, so large headquarters with in-house manufacturing capabilities aren't common. That said, there are an increasing number of performance parts manufacturers and dragster builders setting up business around Europe.

The early pioneers of the sport would build their own chassis on homemade jigs, and British drag racing legends such as Dennis Priddle were incredibly skilled at building early front-engine dragsters, but today the majority of European Top Fuel chassis are imported from America. Without doubt, drag racing is at its most popular in the US, and it's consequently there that most car builders and chassis shops are located. Names such as McKinney (McKinney Corp) and Hadman (Brad Hadman) are amongst those most commonly found as the chassis manufacturer on race entry sheets. In recent years European teams have enjoyed good business relationships with the US teams, procuring state-of-the-art racecars from some of the biggest teams in the business. These may well be cars that have been run for a season or two previously, or perhaps spare cars that may never have even been run in anger.

Two names that I believe to have been pivotal in bringing some of the finest Top Fuel machinery from the US to Europe are those

ABOVE AND BELOW The body panels of the dragster are mounted to the chassis rails by Dzus fasteners, allowing easy removal and refixing when the car's being worked on in the team pit area. *(Mark Skinner)*

of Rune Fjeld and Knut Söderqvist. Rune was himself a successful racer before becoming a team owner. His roots are very much in the 'Funny Car' class of drag racing, where he campaigned a number of cars, first on methanol and later nitro. I believe his first Top Fuel car was purchased in the late '80s from NHRA racer Joe Amato. In 1991 another Amato car was making its way to Europe, this time a double NHRA-winning machine that would go on to be one of the most successful cars in history following its NHRA wins. On European soil it would win three FIA European Top Fuel titles and would feature in the historic side-by-side first European four-second/300mph race, in the hands of Andy Carter. Rune has continued to import a number of chassis and complete cars from some of the best names in the US to this day.

'King Knut' was also very much a Funny Car man, successfully campaigning his Harlan Thompson-driven Budweiser cars all over Europe. He too switched to Top Fuel cars at a similar time to Rune, as the FC class had all but died out on European soil. Knut imported a number of complete cars and chassis from the best in the business, as well as doing a bit of

business in the other direction through his own company, *Carbon By Design*.

I believe that without these two characters in our sport, Top Fuel racing in Europe wouldn't be where it is today. What they enabled racers to do was to step up to the pinnacle class without the need to purchase an entire operation, which is an expensive business. If you wanted to run your own motor in their chassis, or had a chassis but needed running gear, this was a way to make it happen. I'm sure that every possible sort of deal was done by these guys over the years, giving many racers who wouldn't otherwise have had the opportunity to run Top Fuel the chance to fulfil their dreams. Without them there would be far fewer Top Fuel chassis or cars in Europe, and many of those they imported remain in use today. Sadly Knut Söderqvist died in an accident at his home in Thailand on 28 April 2012 after having retired from drag racing.

A Top Fuel chassis can be altered or repaired at any point in its career without the need for buying or building a complete new one. As SFI rules change, a new requirement might be to include additional bracing in the driver's section, or to the front or back end. Tubing grade requirements may also be changed by the SFI for improved safety, or a chassis may simply be at the end of its useful life. For instance, despite having already achieved huge success with the Andersen Racing car in 2008, Andy Carter said that the car handled completely differently in 2009, having been 'front-halved' – meaning that everything from the driver's section forward had been cut away and replaced with new tubing; '09 was consequently his most successful year in competition. As well as being front-halved, a chassis can also be 'back-halved', with the section behind the driver being replaced. There are now a number of racecar builders in the UK and Europe who can perform these updates, as well as building complete chassis.

Roll structure/cage

As mentioned previously, a Top Fuel chassis will break away in front or behind the driver in an accident, leaving the driver's cockpit section intact.

Additional diagonal tubing around the driver means that this section remains strong, and further crossmembers are used over the top

of the driver's legs in a modern car, preventing them from protruding outside of the chassis. Further driver protection is provided by a six-point roll cage, *ie* a cage structure connected to the top chassis rails at six points. The inner surfaces of the cage must also be padded with SFI-specification padding to provide additional protection.

All safety harness mountings are made from a small-diameter tubing that's arch-shaped and tig-welded to the chassis tubes.

The driver's section obviously contains all the driving controls. Rules state that all wiring must be external of the frame rails, but cabling, hydraulic or pneumatic lines may be routed inside the chassis.

As well as the roll cage, all cars must now be fitted with a shroud that completely encloses the rear of the roll cage behind the driver's head. This must be made of either titanium or steel and be moulded round the cage. This new safety measure was introduced following the sad death of US racer Darrell Russell in 2004. He suffered a crash at the top end of the track when his rear tyre blew, causing shrapnel to enter the driver's compartment from the rear, resulting in fatal head injuries.

Fuel tank

The fuel tank has a capacity of 12–15 US gallons, just enough for one pass up the quarter mile while leaving around 1.5 US gallons in the tank. Despite the overall length of the car, its sheer power and traction causes the front end to lift on launch, so to help keep this to a minimum the fuel tank is positioned as far forward as possible to reduce the need for ballast. The fuel then travels through a large-

ABOVE In the event of a crash additional driver protection is provided by a six-point roll cage, the inner surfaces of which are required to be padded with SFI-specification padding. All safety harness mountings are made from small-diameter tubing that's arch-shaped and tig-welded to the chassis tubes. *(Gary Cottingham)*

LEFT An internal view of the driver's section, which contains all the driver controls. All wiring must be external of the frame rails, but cabling and hydraulic or pneumatic lines may be routed inside the chassis. *(Mark Skinner)*

LEFT An external view. *(Mark Skinner)*

LEFT All cars must be fitted with a shroud that completely encloses the rear of the roll cage behind the driver's head, made of either titanium or steel and moulded round the cage. *(Mark Skinner)*

RIGHT The fuel tank has a capacity of 12–15 US gallons, just enough for one pass up the quarter mile run while leaving around 1.5 US gallons in the tank. *(Mark Skinner)*

RIGHT The fuel tank is positioned as far forward as possible to reduce the need for ballast. *(Mark Skinner)*

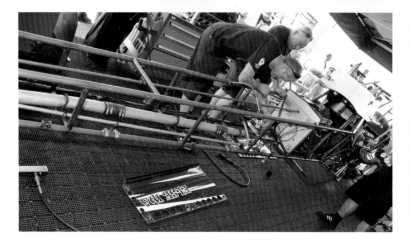

RIGHT AND BELOW The fuel travels through a large-diameter (up to 3in) aluminium pipe that runs the length of the front section and around the driver's seat to the fuel pump. *(Mark Skinner)*

diameter (up to 3in) aluminium pipe that runs the length of the front section and around the driver's seat to the fuel pump.

The tank itself doesn't contain any pump mechanism, so the fuel is drawn from it by an inline fuel pump attached to the front of the engine. G-force on acceleration during a run also aids fuel flow, which is aided in addition by a large breather that protrudes from the top of the fuel tank and through the bodywork, providing a small amount of ram-air effect.

The tank is made from T6 aluminium with baffles built in at manufacture. These baffles prevent the fuel from surging on acceleration and deceleration.

The fuel is made up of nitromethane and methanol, usually to a ratio of 90% nitro to 10% methanol, 90% being the maximum amount of nitro allowed by the regulations. Mixing is done before the fuel is added to the tank, and takes place in a safe, designated area of the team's pit space. It can be carried out as late as the day prior to use, so long as it's shaken before being added to the tank.

There are three ways that the fuel can be mixed: by an airline being placed directly into the fuel jug; by 'pouring the fuel through itself' using two drums – for example, two of the five gallons in one drum are poured into an empty drum, then the two gallons are poured back in with the three gallons, and so on (Top Fuel pioneer Don Garlits always used this method to

BELOW The tank is made from T6 aluminium with baffles built in at manufacture. These baffles prevent the fuel from surging on acceleration and deceleration. *(Mark Skinner)*

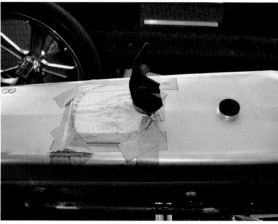

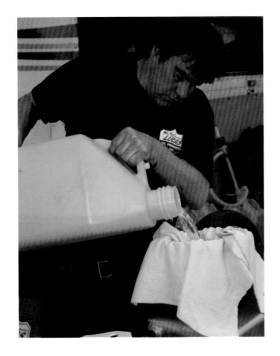

mix his fuel); and finally by simply picking up the fuel container and shaking it!

It's vital that the nitro/methanol percentages used are correct, so a digital gauge is used to measure this. If they aren't right then more of either element is added until the correct percentage is measured.

The fuel mix is stored in five-US-gallon heavy duty plastic fuel jugs. To add the fuel to the dragster an aluminium cap is unscrewed from the top of the tank, a funnel with a fine filter is placed into the opening and the contents of the jug are poured in until around 1in below the neck of the tank.

Wheelie bars

Wheelie bars have been a legal requirement on Top Fuel cars since 2006. Prior to this the class was the only one not to use them, but as the threat of blowovers increased the NHRA took the decision to make them mandatory. A blowover occurs when the front wheels of the dragster lift to a height where air gets underneath the bottom of the car, causing it to go straight up and over. This has fortunately become very rare since the introduction of wheelie bars.

The wheelie bars are fitted to the rear of the dragster, where they're bolted to the chassis at three points. They comprise a triangular structure built from 4130 chromoly tubes with a single wheel at the back. Rules state that

LEFT Wheelie bars are designed to reduce the risk of a blowover, which can occur when the front wheels of the dragster lift to a height that allows air to get underneath the bottom of the car, causing it to go straight up and over. *(Andy Carter Collection)*

the wheelie bars must be a maximum height of 4in measured from the racing surface, and the wheels must be made from a non-metallic product, usually rubber or plastic.

Suspension and steering

Suspension

A Top Fuel dragster has no suspension. The rear axle is bolted directly and solidly to the top and bottom rear chassis rails, and the front A-arms are bolted solidly to the top and bottom front chassis rails. Although rare, some teams choose to tig-weld the front A-arms to the rails.

Steering

Steering wheel

The Top Fuel dragster steering wheel is a far cry from the hugely expensive and complex wheels used in modern Formula 1 cars. It isn't, for instance, collapsible in the event of an accident. It's made from aluminium or carbon fibre and has to have a quick-release mechanism to aid cockpit access and egress by the driver. This mechanism works by the driver pushing a button on the side of the steering hub. The steering wheel is then able to slide on and off of the spline on the steering column.

Often referred to as a butterfly wheel, it must meet SFI spec 42.1, which covers construction material, release mechanism hub and shaft and the required testing of release whilst wearing the approved class racing gloves.

There are usually no buttons or controls, although some drivers choose to mount a pneumatic parachute release button on the steering wheel.

Steering column

The steering column is of one-piece construction, made from chromoly or titanium tubing. It's attached to the steering rack by way of splines and a nut and bolt

ABOVE A Top Fuel dragster steering wheel is a far cry from the hugely expensive and complex wheels used in modern Formula 1 cars. *(Mark Skinner)*

BELOW The steering wheel is made from aluminium or carbon fibre and must have a quick-release mechanism to aid cockpit access and exit for the driver. *(Mark Skinner)*

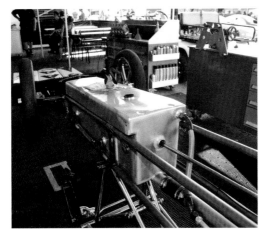

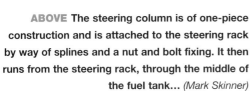

ABOVE The steering column is of one-piece construction and is attached to the steering rack by way of splines and a nut and bolt fixing. It then runs from the steering rack, through the middle of the fuel tank… *(Mark Skinner)*

fixing. It then runs from the steering rack, through the middle of the fuel tank up to the cockpit bulkhead, then through the cockpit bulkhead into the cockpit. Along the way it passes through a support bearing due to its considerable length, as well as a final support bearing in the cockpit.

Steering rack

The steering rack of choice for most teams is the Strange lightweight aluminium rack and pinion unit. The steering rack is a 'slow rack', which is the opposite to the quick rack that's used in most other motorsport disciplines. In other words, turning the steering will only move the front wheels a small amount so as to avoid overcorrection. It has less than a full turn, lock to lock. The steering rack is connected to the track control arms by a rose joint that's secured with a high-tensile shouldered $^3/_8$th UNF bolt.

Track rods

A Top Fuel dragster doesn't use track rods as you'd find on a normal road car. Instead the dragster uses a rose joint to connect to the track control arms. These must be made of either chromoly or titanium. Aluminium track control arms aren't permitted in FIA Top Fuel racing.

ABOVE …up to the cockpit bulkhead… *(Mark Skinner)*

LEFT …and then through the cockpit bulkhead in to the cockpit. *(Mark Skinner)*

BELOW The steering rack of choice for most teams is the Strange lightweight aluminium rack and pinion unit. *(Mark Skinner)*

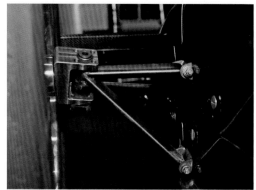

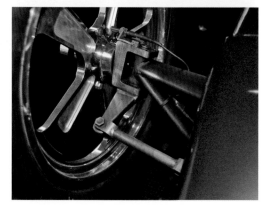

RIGHT The front A-arms are made of chromoly and are bolted to the top and bottom chassis rails. *(Mark Skinner)*

FAR RIGHT Teams carry spare front wheels and A-arms in the race trailer as part of their spares package. *(Mark Skinner)*

RIGHT The steering section viewed from above. *(Mark Skinner)*

FAR RIGHT Here a data logging sensor can also be seen, for measuring front-wheel speed. *(Mark Skinner)*

BELOW The front wheels can be staggered up to a maximum of 3in. This is achieved by mounting the A-arms slightly staggered on each side to increase 'rollout' when you leave the start line. *(Illustration by 3tc)*

A-arms

The front A-arms are made of chromoly and are bolted to the top and bottom chassis rails. The advantage of bolting them is that if the car performs a wheelstand and damages an A-arm, this can be easily replaced, unlike a welding option. Teams carry spare front wheels and A-arms as part of their spares package in the race trailer.

The front wheels can be staggered up to a maximum of 3in. This is achieved by mounting the A-arms slightly staggered on each side. The maximum wheelbase is measured from the furthest wheel forward. This is done to increase 'rollout' when you leave the start line.

Rollout is to do with the staging beams at the start line and how the front wheels break them. It's basically the time between the driver initiating the start movement and the car physically reaching the start-line beam that starts the timing clocks. There are seven variables that can influence rollout, with five controlled by the driver and the other two by the track staff. They'll set up the height of the beams, and if these are too high then rollout is increased, making it harder to pull a red light. Too low and rollout is decreased, in turn increasing the chance of an illegal start and the resulting red light. Traction is also a variable that the track itself can influence – if the surface is too slippery, causing spin, then you'll have a longer rollout.

The five driver-controlled factors are: vehicle weight; how the car is staged (*eg* shallow, middle or deep); clutch slippage; amount of rpm applied at the start; and front-tyre air pressure/tyre diameter.

All of these elements come into play and affect what is a very complicated start-line factor.

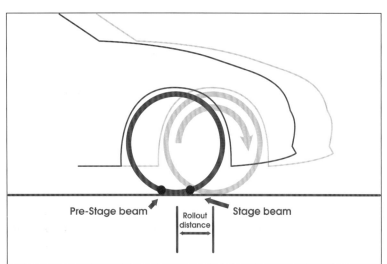

Pre-Stage beam Rollout distance Stage beam

Brakes

As with most high-speed, straight-line vehicles, much like land speed cars a Top Fuel dragster relies on parachutes as its main form of braking.

That said, a Top Fuel dragster does have brakes on the rear wheels. These are controlled not by a pedal but by using a vertical lever in the cockpit. While the parachutes provide the main form of braking at the top end of a run, the rear brakes are used more during the early stages of a run sequence, including the start up, burnout, backing up and staging the car.

During the course of a run a driver can experience traction loss and extreme tyre vibration known as 'tyre shake'. This can sometimes be controlled by applying the brake. Of course, should there be an issue with parachute deployment at speed then braking can be applied to help slow the car. Rules state that braking must be controlled entirely by the

ABOVE A Top Fuel dragster relies on parachutes as its main form of braking. *(Dom Romney)*

LEFT Although the parachutes provide the main form of braking at the top end of a run, the rear brakes are used more during the early stages of a run sequence, including the start-up, burnout, backing up and staging the car. *(Mark Skinner)*

41

ABOVE **Two separate shroud line mountings are required with sleeved, half-inch minimum grade 8 steel bolts with self-locking nuts, or nuts that have been welded on to the parachute brackets.** *(Mark Skinner)*

driver, with no electronic, pneumatic or other devices allowed.

A minimum of two rear-wheel hydraulic disc brakes measuring 11.5in in diameter are required, and carbon-fibre brake rotors must be used with carbon-fibre brake pads – both becoming a mandatory requirement in 2010.

The rear brake calipers are four piston calipers and are made from either magnesium or billet aluminium. The 11in discs are made from carbon fibre and are operated by a single hydraulic circuit. A hand-operated brake lever in the cockpit is attached to a small, single master cylinder that pushes hydraulic Dot 5 brake

fluid through braided, fireproof brake lines to each caliper. The hydraulic brake line is usually run inside the bottom right-hand chassis rail for protection. The calipers are mounted on a bracket over the brake discs.

Braking parachutes

As mentioned previously, a Top Fuel dragster relies on parachutes for braking, the rules stating that two must be used. When deployed these will pull the driver through 6 negative G, so their mounting is of huge importance to avoid them being ripped off. Protection from fire damage is also essential, as they sit right behind the motor. Should anything go wrong on a run resulting in a fire, then the flames will head straight back to the chutes and can burn them off if the fire is large enough.

In terms of mounting requirements, two separate shroud line mountings are required with sleeved, ½in minimum grade 8 steel bolts with self-locking nuts or nuts that have been welded on to the parachute brackets. These mounting brackets must be constructed using a minimum $3/16$in 4130 steel or titanium. The shroud lines themselves are required to be covered with $1/16$in thick leather or other approved material such as Kevlar, from their mounting point into the pack.

Two parachute tethers must then be routed through each shroud line end loop and attached to the rear end mounting bolts on both sides. The tethers are also required to be covered in a fireproof material.

Each chute has its own release lever that's operated by the driver from the cockpit. These are attached to the parachute packs by a thin cable. When the levers are pushed forward, the cable is pulled out of the parachute pack allowing it to open and the parachutes to be deployed. Each chute is attached to a spring-

Drag Chute diagram.
(Illustration by 3tc)

Free length

Skirt band

Loop   Confluence point

Suspension lines

Canopy

Bridle

Drogue

Tow line

Main seam

RIGHT **Each chute has its own release lever (arrowed), operated by the driver from the cockpit.** *(Mark Skinner)*

FAR RIGHT **The packs that contain the parachutes before release.** *(Mark Skinner)*

loaded drogue, which is the first thing to exit the parachute pack.

The parachutes are made of nylon and can be ordered in any colour required. Often a team will opt for a colour that matches their sponsor's colour scheme, and sponsors' names can also be added.

Parachutes are damaged the most from being dragged along the ground as the car slows down at the top end of the track after the run. They are inspected after each run and replaced as required.

The chutes are required to be carefully packed. Before a run many drivers like to inspect this duty as it's performed. For peace of mind some will even pack their own.

A pin is placed in the pack once the chutes are loaded and ready to run. This pin carries a label reading 'Remove before flight'. It will be a crew member's duty to remove these after the burnout is performed and to signal to the crew chief that it's been done before the driver pulls into stage. During extreme vibration caused by tyre shake the cables can sometimes shake out, causing the chutes to deploy on a run.

Wheels and tyres

Wheels

One of the most obvious visual features of a Top Fuel dragster is the contrasting size of the front and rear wheels. Many early dragsters would use wire wheels on the front, but these were found to be too weak and are no longer permitted. The modern front wheel diameter must be a minimum of 17in. Again, both front and rear wheels must conform to SFI specs, with the fronts being required to meet SFI spec 15.2, which controls manufacture standards, safety and impact testing and materials. The front wheels are constructed of forged aluminium.

The front and rear wheels are all constructed of forged aluminium. However, the rear wheels are a hugely important part of a Top Fuel car and are designed to withstand pretty much anything short of a nuclear explosion. They go from sitting idle on the start line to bearing the brunt of 8,000hp and 100mph in under a second, shortly before handling the centrifugal force of spinning at more than 320mph! In 2010 the SFI set about upgrading the rear wheel

FAR LEFT The chutes have been wrapped around the rear wing at the end of the run to stop them becoming tangled up on the journey back to the pit area. Note the tape over the wheelie bars to prevent the chutes getting caught on release. *(Mark Skinner)*

LEFT The chutes are required to be carefully packed. Before a run many drivers like to inspect this duty as it's performed – some will even pack their own for peace of mind. *(Mark Skinner)*

FAR LEFT The modern front-wheel diameter must be a minimum of 17in and be spindle-mounted. *(Mark Skinner)*

LEFT The rear wheels are a hugely important part of a Top Fuel car and are designed to withstand pretty much anything short of a nuclear explosion. *(Mark Skinner)*

spec from 15.3 to 15.4, following an increase in performance of the nitro classes. This is now the legal requirement of the NHRA. The wheels must be 16in beadlock design with a minimum inner bead of 14¾in. This means that a part of the wheel rim fits round the bead of the tyre. The bolt-on beadlock ring must be made of 7075-T6 aluminium with a minimum yield strength of 65,000psi and a minimum tensile strength of 75,000psi. The beadlock receiver

rings and bolt-on rings must have a maximum outer diameter of 17¼in. The bolt-on rings must then be retained by 24–28 fasteners which must be a minimum of ⁵/₁₆in. The minimum material under the beadlock ring bolt heads must be 0.300in thick. SFI 15.4 spec requires modular wheels to have a centre bolt load distribution ring manufactured from 4130 steel 0.125in thick sandwiching the rim shell flanges between the ring and the wheel centre. One manufacturer is currently developing a one-piece forged wheel that meets the required specification. Any modifications or lightening of both the front and rear wheels is prohibited along with the use of titanium wheel studs.

Rear wheels are secured to the rear axle hubs by five wheel nuts. The studs are ½in in diameter and the aluminium alloy nuts are torqued up to 110ft/lb. Front wheels are spindle mounted.

Tyre history

A modern Top Fuel dragster has no tread on either the front or rear tyres it uses, but races only slicks. Dragster slicks were first manufactured professionally in 1958 after early pioneers found bald street tyres provided the best adhesion to the road. Constant tyre development by Goodyear in compounds and fitting has resulted in hugely improved performance, increasing speeds and lowering elapsed times. Modern Top Fuel dragsters are now limited to one tyre choice – the Goodyear Eagle Dragway Special.

Rear tyres

The rear tyres are a monstrous 36.0 x 17.5–16 and are nearly 10ft in circumference. Monster rubber comes with an equally monstrous price tag of around $900 per tyre, and they only last for a mile – around four passes!

They're designed to change in diameter and width as speed increases. The static diameter of 36in will expand to 60in whilst the 18in width will shrink to between 10–12in. In effect this change provides a variable gear ratio at speed.

The walls of the tyres are designed to wrinkle upon acceleration. The rim of the wheel wants to turn faster than the tyre on initial acceleration, and the sidewalls' give is referred to as 'wrapping'. When the tyre is wrapped, its contact with the track is as long as it is wide, providing maximum traction. Once the car has left the line the tyres quickly start to gain in height, resulting in a narrowed contact with the racing surface. It's as this process begins that tyre shake can occur. This is caused by the tyre not unwrapping itself smoothly; instead it begins to roll over itself whilst slapping the ground, causing violent shaking of the car. Tyre shake is a nightmare for the driver, and in extreme cases racers have been knocked unconscious by the vibration. Vision is completely obscured and a headache usually follows!

As the tyre grows in height during the pass and the contact area decreases, the rear wing does its job of maintaining traction by applying the downforce required to help the tyres stick to the track.

The minimum air pressure allowed at the start of a run is 6.5psi, and this will be checked and set by a crew member whilst the car is towed down to the start line. Tyres are inflated using normal air supplied by a compressor.

The tyres are rated to 350mph and are of radial pattern and steel belted. They're inspected visually after every run for abrasion or damage such as cuts.

Front tyres

The front tyres are 3in in width and are mounted on a 17in wheel. Tyre pressures vary between 70–100psi depending on driver

LEFT Here crew members can be seen fitting new rubber, which is a two-man job. *(Gary Cottingham)*

LEFT The rear tyres are a monstrous 36.0 x 17.5–16 and are nearly 10ft in circumference. They only last for one mile – about four passes! *(Gary Cottingham)*

LEFT The tyres are rated to 350mph, are of radial pattern and are steel belted. Tyres are inspected visually after every run for abrasion or damage such as cuts. *(Gary Cottingham)*

FAR LEFT The rear tyres' static diameter of 36in will expand to 60in whilst their 18in width will shrink to between 10–12in. This change in effect provides a variable gear ratio at speed. *(Gary Cottingham)*

LEFT The minimum air pressure allowed at the start of a run is 6.5psi. This is checked and set by a crew member whilst the car is towed down to the start line. *(Gary Cottingham)*

ABOVE **The front tyres are 3in in width and are mounted on a 17in wheel.** (Mark Skinner)

coming from a fabric carcass made primarily from nylon, which allows for the tyres' required transformation.

Tyre wear is measured by small holes in the rubber that allow a team to gauge how much life is left before a change is required. However, most teams will have a maximum run number which is usually around a mile, or four passes, and will change it at this point. Old tyres are often put up for sale in the pits as souvenirs for hardened race enthusiasts.

Tyre warming and temperatures

Although tyre-warming products are available for Top Fuel dragsters, the burnout itself is used as the main way of adding temperature to the rear slicks. This procedure involves the car driving through a small amount of water and then spinning the tyres, causing them to smoke. During this process the temperature will rise to around 120°C.

The trick is to then keep the heat in the tyre by reversing the car back in the rubber tracks that you've just created. As well as adding heat, old compound is scrubbed off, as well as laying down fresh rubber on the racing surface for added traction. After a run the tyre temperature will have increased to between 250°C and 400°C.

preference. On launch the front tyres have a much easier ride, as the front wheels are often airborne for 60ft or so! These tyres are also rated to 350mph and will usually last for around 20 passes or five miles.

Construction and compounds

The tyres are constructed using a compound called D2A, which is very heat resistant and hard wearing. The tread depth on a new tyre is around 0.20in at the centre. The rubber compound provides less than 1% of the tyre structure, with almost all the remaining structure

RIGHT **The burnout is used as the main way of adding temperature to the rear slicks. During this process the temperature will rise to around 120°C.** (Dom Romney)

Aerodynamics

The modern Top Fuel dragster owes most of its aero design to years of on-track development, rather than endless man-hours in a wind tunnel. If you were to compare a '70s rear-engine car with its modern-day equivalent the general appearance remains similar – long chassis design, large rear tyres with an equally large rear wing overhead, small front wheels and a form of wing at the front.

As has been the case throughout Top Fuel dragster history, Don Garlits has been a front-runner. Having already pioneered the successful rear-engine dragster, it was Garlits who introduced the rear wing, recognising the importance of downforce on the rear tyres. Soon after this innovation all fuel dragsters added their own wings, as well as many trying forms of wing on the sides of the car, with little success.

Added weight will always be one of the biggest issues for Top Fuel dragster aerodynamics, in what is essentially a raw power motorsport. If you add additional aerodynamics you add to the weight of the car, with some of the '80s pioneers suggesting weight gains of up to 250lb.

Garlits was again very much at the forefront of a very brief 'aero race' in the '80s, but like most things from that decade, much of this development was best left there! In 1986 the NHRA increased the class minimum weight by 100lb. This, along with technological developments in materials, such as carbon fibre and Kevlar, meant that a small number of teams would introduce a number of streamlining ideas before the close of the 1987 season.

Gary Ormsby was a major player at this time, due in no small part to major backing from oil giant Castrol. With the budget in the bank and a team of engineers on hand, he set about developing a revolutionary new streamlined body. Key features were a lower front end sweeping up towards the driver's cockpit, and additional styling over the top of a sunken roll cage. Full side-pods were also introduced enclosing the headers and pushing air around the rear tyres. The motor was barely visible, with the rear section almost completely enclosed. The rear wing structure was left untouched.

Garlits, on the other hand, didn't have the

engineers or the technology. He simply had his years of experience dealing with wings and planes and reading books. His design for Swamp Rat 30 was more about the front end, where he created a teardrop-shaped nose that fully enclosed the front wheels, preventing them from disturbing airflow. He also introduced a full canopy over the driver, completely enclosing the cockpit. In essence, his design changes were relatively small in comparison to the Ormsby car; for Garlits it was more about cleaning the car up, and he achieved this without adding extra weight. Whilst it's believed Garlits' new

ABOVE Don Garlits was very much at the forefront of a very brief 'aero race' in the 1980s. *(Don Garlits Collection)*

BELOW Garlits' design for Swamp Rat 30 was more about the front end, where he created a tear-drop-shaped nose that fully enclosed the front wheels, preventing them from disturbing airflow. He also introduced a full canopy over the driver, completely enclosing the cockpit. *(Don Garlits Collection)*

nose weighed around 4lb, some of the other streamlined bodies were piling on the pounds, with the heaviest adding around 400lb.

During the 1986 season both Garlits and Ormsby had their teething troubles, but it was Garlits who enjoyed the greater success, qualifying number 1 and smashing through the 270mph barrier during his first outing in the car, and winning the event.

Garlits would go on to record many more event wins and conclude the season nearly 5,000 points ahead of Ormsby, who struggled to even make the top ten all year. However, it wasn't completely straightforward for Garlits, who having set the national record at

ABOVE The carbon fibre front wing is single element and adjustable. It's mounted to the chassis by chromoly brackets that protrude out from the underside of the wing. *(Gary Cottingham)*

BELOW The front wing must be no more than 63in wide in total. *(Mark Skinner)*

Englishtown found himself held on the start line during the next run, which lightened the fuel load enough to allow air under the front end at launch. The air caught underneath the large nose, pulling the car up and over in what's known as a blowover.

Ormsby would soon revert to a conventional design and find himself competitive again, whilst Garlits continued with the design for his new Swamp Rat 31. Other racers such as Darrell Gwynn, Joe Amato and Gene Snow all tried their hand at streamlining with a limited degree of success, and by mid-1987 the aero development phase was coming to a close.

This very brief era of aerodynamic development was probably described best by one of the pioneers, Gary Ormsby: 'We tried and learned that aerodynamic things that should work, according to theory and computer findings, don't necessarily work on these dragsters. The fastest and quickest cars are conventional dragsters. The bottom line is that drag racing is a horsepower sport. What really makes these cars go is that piece of aluminium between the frame rails. Unlike IndyCar racing, where there's a smooth transition to high speeds, drag racing is a sport of such violent horsepower that many aerodynamic techniques don't apply. Aerodynamics still play a role, but not as much as pure horsepower.'

So what does make an effective difference to a Top Fuel dragster's aerodynamics? By design, a dragster isn't the most aerodynamic vehicle on the planet, with its large exposed engine and open front and rear wheels. But the modern dragster is about as clean as it can be, given that it needs the huge front and rear wings to provide the downforce and stability at the high speeds being achieved.

Front wing

The carbon fibre front wing is single element, and is adjustable. Usually parameters for adjustment are from 0°–8°. The wing is mounted to the chassis by chromoly brackets that protrude out from the underside of the wing.

Rules state that the front wing must be no more than 63in wide in total. The spill plates must be flat, vertical, and both the outer and

inner surfaces must be parallel. These are to be no wider than 0.55in.

Rear wing

The modern rear wing is a carbon fibre triple element design, and provides the essential downforce required on to the huge rear tyres. In the second half of a run the downforce provided will usually be around 8,000lb. Without this the tyres wouldn't be able to maintain the traction level that's required at the top end of the track.

The main supports for the rear wing consist of a very heavy-duty cross-braced wing stand. This is mounted directly to the axle plates at the bottom and to the underside of the rear wing at the top. Two wing stand supports then go from the top, front-side of the stand and then forward to the top of the rear chassis rails. These connect near the rear motor plate, as this is a very strong section of the car's rear. All wing stand material is made from 4130 chromoly aero tubing. All connections – ie to the axle plates, to the wing itself and to the top chassis rails – are by way of shouldered titanium bolts.

Adjustment is made by means of two chromoly tubes that attach to the middle of the main wing stand and the rear lower element of the wing. Lengthening these bars will raise the angle of attack, whereas shortening them will lower it. The angle is measured by an angle gauge that's placed on a flat surface of the wing.

All wing settings must be done prior to any run, as devices that control the wing angle on a pass aren't allowed. The modern wing must also have two independent cables wrapped

around each end of the main element, which are connected to the parachute release cables. This means that if the main element is broken away from its supports, or if either end is broken off, the parachutes will automatically deploy.

The total area of the wing is restricted to a minimum of 1,450in^2 and a maximum of 1,500. The trailing edge must not extend more than 50in behind the centre line of the rear axle. The maximum height as measured from the trailing edge to the ground must be no greater than 90in. Spill plates must be flat, with inner and outer surfaces parallel. Their thickness must be no greater than 0.65in, fitted at right angles to

ABOVE LEFT The spill plates must be flat, vertical, and the outer and inner surfaces must be parallel. *(Mark Skinner)*

ABOVE The modern rear wing is a carbon fibre, triple element design and provides the essential downforce required on to the huge rear tyres. *(Gary Cottingham)*

LEFT The main supports for the rear wing consist of a very heavy-duty, cross-braced wing stand. This is mounted directly to the axle plates at the bottom and to the underside of the rear wing at the top. *(Mark Skinner)*

ABOVE The total area of the wing is restricted to a minimum of 1,450in^2 and a maximum of 1,500. *(Mark Skinner)*

RIGHT The body panels of the car are made of magnesium and carbon fibre. These are then connected to the chassis by Dzus fasteners for easy removal. *(Mark Skinner)*

RIGHT NACA ducts are permitted within the bodywork. Two of these are located facing forward on the top body panel, in the cockpit area just in front of the windscreen. They force air into the cockpit area to stop a build-up of negative pressure. *(Gary Cottingham)*

the wing, and their overall size must fit within the confines of a box 22in x 22in.

Rules state that the wing must be positioned with a positive 2° angle maximum relative to the racing surface, with no minimum.

Body panels

The body panels are made of magnesium and carbon fibre. These are then connected to the chassis by Dzus fasteners for easy removal. The front overhang is measured from the centre of the front wheel spindle and must not exceed 30in. A drivers' windscreen is allowed, which helps to push the airflow, as well as liquids or foreign matter, over their heads. It may be as high as possible without affecting the driver's forward view.

NACA ducts

NACA ducts are permitted within the bodywork. A NACA duct is a low-drag inlet that was originally designed in the US by the National Advisory Committee for Aeronautics (NACA). A Top Fuel dragster will usually have at least four NACA ducts moulded within the body panels. Two of these are usually halfway along the bodywork within the side panels, one mounted on either side. These face rearwards and allow air that could become trapped within the bodywork to escape, and therefore reduce the build-up of air pressure (drag). It's worth mentioning that a Top Fuel dragster has no underside floor tray, so air can flow under the car and become trapped.

Two NACA ducts are also mounted facing forward on the top body panel. These are in the cockpit area just in front of the windscreen. They force air into the cockpit area to stop a build-up of negative pressure. (Negative pressure can aid a fire in the event of flames coming forward into the cockpit area from a burning engine.)

Driver canopies

Top Fuel driver canopies were a feature of the aero wars of the '80s but have seen very little use until recent times. During the 2012 season the NHRA finally allowed the use of driver safety canopies after the pioneering efforts of multi-NHRA Top Fuel champion Tony Schumacher. Much like the canopy of a fighter jet, this new evolution in design is more about driver safety, offering little in the way of aerodynamic advantage.

A Top Fuel dragster canopy is a quick-release unit that pivots upwards at the front to allow access and egress. They're made from clear Lexan, which is a brand name for polycarbonate sheet and resin, available in a variety of grades. Lexan is commonly used for aircraft canopies and is the perfect material for this type of application. Although not a mandatory requirement in Top Fuel, a number of teams are using canopies and continuing to develop them.

Many other forms of motorsport are considering some form of canopy following a number of high-profile incidents where head injuries have been a major factor. In Formula 1, Felipe Massa suffered serious head injuries when he was struck by a component from Rubens Barrichello's Brawn which penetrated his helmet. Not long before this incident, Formula 2 racer Henry Surtees was struck in the head by a loose wheel, which sadly claimed his life; and more recently IndyCar hero Dan Wheldon lost his life following head injuries sustained by hitting a fence support post. It's therefore hoped that this new Top Fuel innovation will aid driver protection, and it'll be interesting to see if other open-cockpit forms of motorsport will follow suit.

Electronics

The use of electronics on a Top Fuel car is limited to the following: ignition systems, data recorders, electrical gauges or indicators, automated fire extinguisher (enclosed cockpit only), fuel system, clutch control and engine shut-off components. Electrical/electronic timers to control pneumatic fuel system valves and/or electric fuel control solenoid valves and/or clutch control valves are also allowed.

Ignition switch
All cars must have a positive on/off switch that can de-energise the entire ignition system. This must be mounted within easy reach of the dragster driver.

Battery
The only battery on board a Top Fuel dragster is a small 12V unit that's used by the data logger and also runs the electronic management

LEFT During the 2012 season the NHRA finally allowed the use of driver safety canopies after the pioneering efforts of multi-NHRA Top Fuel champion Tony Schumacher. *(Gary Cottingham)*

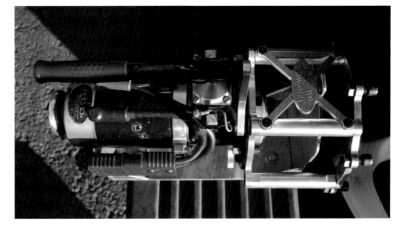

ABOVE There's no driver-operated starter on a Top Fuel dragster. Starting the motor is done by crew members externally, using a large starter motor that's attached to the top pulley on the front of the blower. *(Mark Skinner)*

systems. The only other batteries are external and power the external starter motor as described above.

Radio communications
Radio communications are allowed in Top Fuel dragsters. These allow for two-way conversations between the crew chief and the driver. As you can imagine, this is used prior to a run and after the car is clicked off at the top end of the track. The crew chief will use it prior to the run to inform the driver of how the other teams are performing ahead of their own pass. He'll also use it to relay any information on situations such as oil or other fluids being dropped in one of the lanes, as well as other track conditions. If there's been some kind of accident then this will also be relayed so that the driver knows they can relax for a while ahead of their pass. There could well be instructions relayed on car set-up changes too. At tracks like Santa Pod the pairing lanes run parallel to the track but behind the tower

RIGHT Radio communications are allowed in Top Fuel dragsters. These allow for two-way conversations between the crew chief and the driver. *(Gary Cottingham)*

building at the start as well as grandstands. Consequently as the driver waits they'll have no view of any track action until they're sat directly behind the start ready to run.

The crew chief will often go on ahead of the team to inspect the lanes prior to their pass. Anything he can pass back to the driver before the run can be done via the radio.

At the top end the crew chief can relay times and speeds over the radio so that the driver knows instantly how good a run has been, without having to wait for the crew to arrive with the information.

Cockpit display

The cockpit display is limited, as there's no time to look at this on the run itself. The display is used more in the warm-up and for checks prior to the run, and supplies information to the driver and crew chief on items such as rpm, oil pressure, fuel pressure and time running. There's a light that can be turned on by a switch for use on night runs.

Data logging

In recent years the data logger has become a key piece of equipment in the tuning of Top Fuel cars. However, the information is only as good as the person reading it. Sensor logging will

ABOVE The cockpit display is used more in the warm-up and for checks prior to the run than on the run itself. The driver and crew chief can monitor items such as rpm, oil pressure, fuel pressure and time running. *(Mark Skinner)*

BELOW In recent years the data logger has become a key piece of equipment in tuning a Top Fuel car. *(Mark Skinner)*

BELOW RIGHT Sensor logging provides feedback on fuel volume, fuel pressure, fuel return flow, manifold boost pressure, exhaust gas temperatures, engine rpm, clutch position, clutch temperature, clutch pressure, output shaft speed, front wheel speed, throttle pedal position, ignition timing curve, oil pressure and G meter. *(Mark Skinner)*

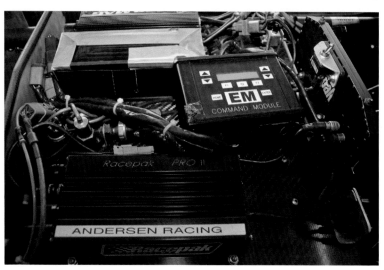

provide feedback on fuel volume, fuel pressure, fuel return flow, manifold boost pressure, exhaust gas temperatures, engine rpm, clutch position, clutch temperature, clutch pressure, output shaft speed, front wheel speed, throttle pedal position, ignition timing curve, oil pressure and the G meter.

After a run this information is downloaded on to a PC in the team's trailer for the crew chief to analyse. The driver will usually have a briefing with the crew chief after each run to provide their own feedback too. This, combined with the information from the data logger and the previous elapsed times of opponents, will help to decide the tune-up for the next run.

One of the most important things gained from the data is the fact that all the systems are working. For example, analysis of the data can show if a mag, coil or ignition box is down, whether the clutch release bearing is moving or if good oil pressure was achieved on a run, etc. The data logger has consequently become a major tool for any Top Fuel team.

Wiring and connectors

The wiring and connectors used on a Top Fuel dragster must survive an extremely hostile environment, and be capable of withstanding extreme vibration as well as very great heat. The

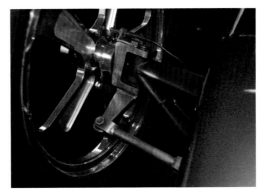

wiring harnesses are designed to be as light as possible and are also screened to guard against electrical interference from the huge dual magnetos. Bespoke wiring looms are made for the car. These must be produced to a very high standard and to tight tolerances in order to ensure a good fit.

Cockpit controls

Unlike most other forms of motorsport, the Top Fuel dragster cockpit is usually home to the driver for a very short period of time (though this can change when there's been an accident or 'oil down' in the preceding race; then a driver might end up strapped in for up to 30 minutes, waiting for the track to be made race-ready again). Due to their extra weight and

the actual time and speed of a run, complicated manual controls or displays are therefore kept to a minimum, and generally include only the steering wheel, throttle pedal, clutch pedal, brake lever, forward/reverse lever, parachute release lever, fuel pump lever, mag switches and data logger switches.

Cockpit display
Top Fuel dragsters use a Racepak liquid-crystal display unit mounted directly in front of the

driver. This is part of the data logging system, and is used by the crew to check the engine rpm, fuel pressure, oil pressure and run time during the warm-up and prior to staging the car.

Steering wheel
See 'Suspension and steering'.

Pedals
There are only two pedals on a Top Fuel dragster: accelerator and clutch. All other controls are performed by levers. The pedals are made from T6 billet aluminium, titanium or magnesium, and are sometimes powder-coated. The accelerator pedal will usually have a small heel plate as well as a loop over the toe area to help keep the foot in place. Underneath the throttle pedal is an air switch which, when depressed, will actuate the car's clutch timers, fuel timers and magneto map. This switch is pneumatic and made from brass. The total accelerator pedal travel is around 3in, although this depends on driver preference.

The throttle pedal is connected to the injector hat by way of a single, heavy-duty Bowden cable that runs from the side of the pedal, along the chassis rail and up past the magnetos to the injector hat. (A Bowden cable is a flexible cable used to transmit mechanical force or energy through the movement of an inner cable – most often steel or stainless steel – housed in an outer cable housing. The housing is usually of composite construction, consisting of a helical steel wire, lined with nylon and with a plastic outer sheath.)

The clutch pedal is of heavy-duty design and is connected by a chromoly rod that runs from the pedal, alongside the lower-left chassis rail, out from the rear of the cockpit. It then passes the engine to a bell-crank mounted inside the chassis rail in the vicinity of the clutch can. Another small rod connects the bell-crank to the clutch arm. All connections in this assembly are rose-jointed. The entire clutch mechanism is mechanical and is operated by the driver's left foot. The clutch pedal operation involves no hydraulics at all.

Other cockpit-mounted controls
As mentioned under 'Pedals', there is no brake pedal, so the carbon fibre rear brakes are

operated by a long lever located on the right-hand side of the cockpit. This is made from either aluminium or carbon fibre.

There is no manual gear change mechanism other than a lever used to engage reverse and forward (there is no neutral on a Top Fuel dragster, which is always in forward or reverse). This lever is mounted on the left side of the cockpit and is made of aluminium or carbon fibre. It's connected to the reverser by a heavy-duty Bowden cable that runs alongside the lower-left chassis rail.

After the burnout procedure prior to the run

On the top left chassis rail on the left side of the cockpit is mounted a lever that controls the massive fuel pump – pull back on the lever and the pump is fully open, while pushing it forward turns the pump off. The fuel pump lever is made of aluminium or carbon fibre and is connected to the fuel pumps by two heavy-duty Bowden cables.

During start-up and burnout the lever is set around half open, which provides enough fuel and fuel pressure to perform the short warm-up, burnout, back-up and going into pre-stage. Once in pre-stage the lever is pulled all the way back and the driver's foot is released from the clutch pedal. This is referred to as going on to the 'high side'. Mounted on the top chassis rail on the right side are two further levers, one to deploy each parachute. Somewhere within easy reach of the driver will be a kill switch to turn off the magnetos after a run or in the event of an emergency.

Safety equipment

Despite the huge speeds associated with drag racing, the sport has a very good safety record. This is in no small part due to the efforts of the SFI, NHRA, MSA, FIA and other governing bodies, who constantly strive to make the sport as safe as possible. Every effort is made to protect the driver in the eventuality that something goes wrong, from driver clothing to bullet-proof blankets designed to catch debris from a damaged motor. The modern Top Fuel driver must wear a full-face racing helmet; fire-resistant head sock and helmet skirt; fire-resistant underwear, gloves, socks and boots; as well as a full firesuit made from Nomex or similar material.

ABOVE On the left side of the cockpit, mounted on the top-left chassis rail, is a lever (arrowed) that controls the massive fuel pump. (Mark Skinner)

LEFT There's no brake pedal, so the carbon fibre rear brakes are operated by a long lever (arrowed) located on the right side of the cockpit. (Mark Skinner)

LEFT The modern Top Fuel driver must wear a full-face racing helmet, fire-resistant head sock and helmet skirt, and fire-resistant underwear, gloves, socks and boots, as well as a full firesuit made from Nomex or similar material.

(Gary Cottingham)

A seven-point, quick-release safety harness holds the driver in place, and arm restraints must be worn. The helmet must be fitted with a HANS (head and neck support) device and, as mentioned earlier, the driver's head is also protected by a titanium shield at the rear of the roll cage.

The SFI spec padding on the roll cage and strengthened driver's chassis section provide protection in the event of a crash, and the cage and driver's section are designed to break away from the rest of the chassis. Other safety features include on-board fire extinguishers (enclosed cockpit cars only), Kevlar blankets around the supercharger, oil pan and reverser, titanium shielding around the clutch, damage-resistant fuel tank, lines and fittings, as well as externally accessible fuel and ignition shut-offs designed to be accessible by safety crew members.

There are a number of Top Fuel dragster crashes every season in the US, where the driver often just walks away. Andy Carter suffered very few major incidents in his time as a Top Fuel driver, but in 2003, whilst racing in Norway, he lost a rear tyre at around 280mph. Despite the damage to the car, Andy walked away and was soon back in the pits trying to source another chassis so that hc could complete the event! Many UK fans will recall the heart-stopping moment when TF legend Barry Sheavills found himself a passenger as his car broke in half at similar speeds whilst going through the finish line at Santa Pod Raceway. Again, despite his car being completely destroyed Barry was able to walk away and was back in the

pits soon after, chatting to fans about the incident and selling bits of the car as souvenirs. These and many similar incidents are testimony to the safety of a modern Top Fuel dragster.

Fire extinguishers

Top Fuel dragsters must be fitted with an on-board fire-extinguishing system if the cockpit is enclosed. This type of system has a nozzle pointing at the engine, a nozzle pointing at the driver and is activated manually by means of a button or pull-lever should the driver require. These must meet SFI regulation 17.1, which states manufacturer options that can be used as well as certification requirements. Each system must carry the relevant SFI labels to be deemed legal and must be checked every two years. Their overall age must not exceed six years.

Electrical shut-off

The 2010 season brought a new safety device to Top Fuel. Should the rear wing collapse, a burst panel break or the driver be rendered unable to perform the normal shutdown sequence at the conclusion of a run, a pair of redundant transmitters, placed 400ft and 600ft past the finish line, will signal an on-board control that will automatically shut off ignition and fuel to the engine and deploy the parachutes. This on-board controller receives power from the existing 12V battery pack already used on the car.

The transmitters are designed and placed so as to avoid inadvertent triggering of the automated shut-offs. These transmitters and the safety shut-off controller were designed by NHRA's Track Safety Committee and constructed by Electrimotion, and are a direct result of Scott Kalitta's death. In Europe the trackside transmitters aren't used, but all the shut-off systems (ignition, fuel and parachutes) must be fitted to the dragster; these are then manually triggered by the driver if needed. I'm sure that it's only a matter of time before the US system is introduced to Europe.

Driver's harness

The driver is strapped into the car with a seven-point, 3in-wide quick-release harness. A seven-point system consists of two shoulder straps, two pelvic straps, two leg straps and one crotch strap. All of these connect to one central

BELOW **The 2010 season brought a new safety device to Top Fuel – an on-board safety shut-off controller that will automatically shut off ignition and fuel to the engine and deploy the parachutes.** *(Illustration by 3tc)*

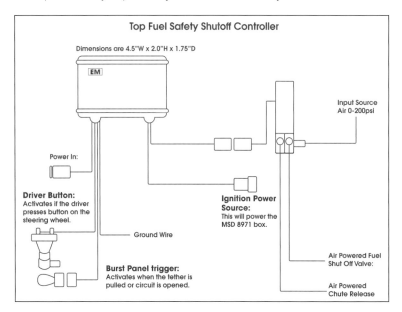

Top Fuel Safety Shutoff Controller

Dimensions are 4.5"W x 2.0"H x 1.75"D

EM

Input Source
Air 0-200psi

Power In:

Driver Button:
Activates if the driver presses button on the steering wheel.

Ground Wire

Burst Panel trigger:
Activates when the tether is pulled or circuit is opened.

Ignition Power Source:
This will power the MSD 8971 box.

Air Powered Fuel Shut Off Valve:

Air Powered Chute Release

quick-release buckle. The straps are secured to mounting brackets that are tig-welded to the chassis. The harness needs to be as tight as possible and is therefore secured by one of the crew prior to the run. A tool is often used to tighten the belt as much as possible.

All belts are required to have a fire-resistant covering and must be updated every two years from the date of manufacture.

Arm restraints

Arm restraints are required to keep the driver's arms within the confines of the cockpit in case of an accident. These are secured around the driver's forearms and to the central buckle of the harness.

Driver's seat

The seat is made of carbon fibre and is held in place by Dzus fasteners. Slots in the seat allow for the harness to feed through, over and around the driver. A foam energy-absorbing material is placed on this and then formed to the driver. This is covered with a minimum one layer of flame-retardant material. Magnesium is not permitted.

HANS device

All drivers are required to wear a HANS device ('head and neck support'), which protects the head and neck and reduces the likelihood of serious injury. Usually made from carbon fibre, the U-shaped device consists of a yoke that fits over the driver's shoulders and under the shoulder straps of the seven-point harness. Two tethers, one on each side of the head, buckle it to the helmet. Again, an SFI label is required to show the device conforms to approved specifications.

Driver's clothing

The modern Top Fuel clothing requirement is a far cry from the early years of racing when drivers would sit behind nitro-burning motors in a T-shirt or jacket! These days driver safety is a priority, and a seven-layer Nomex suit is required.

Nomex was developed in the '60s and is an aramid plastic fabric that's used by firefighters as well as racers. The driver's firesuit can be either a one-piece option similar in style to the type of suit used in most other forms of motorsport, or a two-piece consisting of

ABOVE The helmet must be fitted with a HANS (head and neck support) device. *(Gary Cottingham)*

LEFT Driver safety is a priority, so a seven-layer Nomex suit is required. The driver's firesuit can be a one-piece option similar in style to the type of suit used in most other forms of motorsport or a two-piece consisting of trousers and jacket. *(Gary Cottingham)*

trousers and jacket. A two-piece suit must have a minimum 8in overlap in the waist area. All cuffs and closures, such as zips or Velcro, must be of a fire-resistant or retardant construction. Each suit must be SFI certified, and only permitted manufacturer clothing is allowed. Once certified, the suit must then be retested and certified every five years.

One SFI-approved manufacturer is Simpson, founded by the legendary Bill Simpson. In an advertising campaign for his safety wear, Simpson famously set himself alight wearing one of his firesuits, proving the faith he had in his product.

Nomex SFI-approved gloves, boots/shoes, head sock (balaclava), helmet skirt and underwear must also be worn.

RIGHT An iconic piece of drag racing design and imagery – the classic open-face helmet with a fireproof breather mask underneath. (Don Ewald)

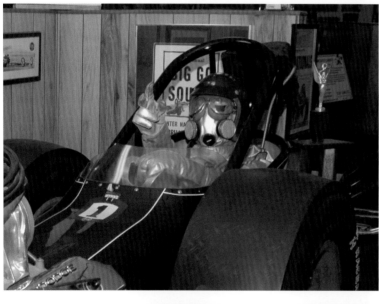

BELOW Two large breathers act as a filter against nitro fumes that are forced back towards the driver of old front-engined cars. (Gary Cottingham)

Driver's helmet

The classic Top Fuel helmet is an iconic piece of drag racing design and imagery. The classic choice consists of an open-face helmet with a fireproof breather mask underneath. A key feature of this type of mask is the two large breathers that sit either side of the lower face area and act as a filter against the nitro fumes that are forced back towards the driver of the old front-engined cars. This nostalgic style is used today by many racers in other classes, as well as fuel racers in the nostalgia classes that are currently so popular in drag racing. Some modern helmets reflect this design style by the introduction of breather filters on the front.

All current racers must use a full-face helmet meeting Snell standards SA2000, SA2005 or SA2010 or 31.2A. Snell standards came about after the death of amateur motorsport racer Pete Snell, who died from head injuries sustained during a crash in the 1950s. His friends founded the organisation to improve the safety standard of protective helmets. All helmets undergo vigorous testing for penetration, impact and crushing before they obtain the required Snell approval.

Dragster helmets are designed to be as light as possible, with most being constructed from carbon fibre covered in a reinforced resin. If the helmet includes a breather system then the internal respirators will enclose the mouth and nose area, to filter fuel and other debris. Some

BELOW The driver's head is also protected by a titanium shield at the rear of the roll cage. (Mark Skinner)

RIGHT All current racers must use a full-face helmet, with most being constructed from carbon fibre covered in a reinforced resin. (Gary Cottingham)

Thomas Nataas

designs include a built-in head sock and skirt, negating the need for individual items. All internal padding provides driver comfort and must have a fire-resistant covering. Chin-straps must also be fire retardant, with most being made from Kevlar and using locking D-rings for closure. Some helmets have an additional D-ring on the chin area to help keep the head secure during a hard launch. All Top Fuel helmets must be fitted with HANS device buckles.

All visors are made from polycarbonate. They provide good visibility and a high level of impact protection.

Engine

The Top Fuel dragster engine is a very distinctive and beautiful piece of engineering, and the fact that it's fully exposed allows for a unique view of the power plant through its good moments and its bad: the good – inlet butterflies on the injector hat wide open at full throttle with nitro flames bursting from the headers; the bad – unburnt fuel streaming from a header as a cylinder fails to fire, or a full engine explosion with a mass of flame trailing behind.

ABOVE LEFT AND ABOVE Other safety features include Kevlar blankets around the supercharger and titanium shielding around the clutch. *(Mark Skinner)*

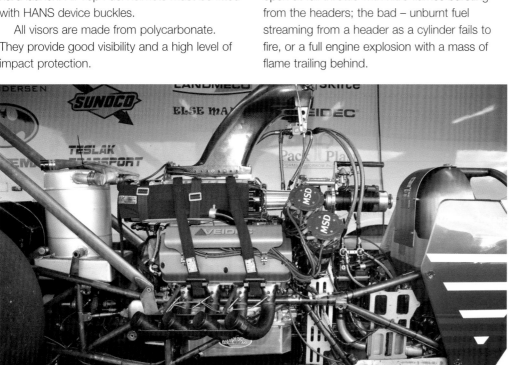

LEFT The Top Fuel dragster engine is a very distinctive and beautiful piece of engineering. *(Mark Skinner)*

The appearance of the engine is quite unique to drag racing. The large engine block sits centrally, with a massive cylinder head each side; a huge supercharger sits between the cylinder heads, and on top of that is a massive carbon fibre injector hat, all flanked by two large banks of headers that breathe fire during a run.

Similar outward views of a fuel motor can be witnessed throughout drag racing's various other classes, but in a smaller configuration.

The modern Top Fuel dragster engine is very loosely based on the Chrysler Hemi 426in[3] 'Elephant Engine'. The current motors still resemble their retro Hemi relation, but in terms of modern technology and output there's a huge gulf between them. The '60s fuel-burning motors were putting out around 1,000bhp, which is pretty impressive. However, the modern TF power plant produces around 8,000!

The engine still has hemispherical combustion chambers, retaining the original basic configuration, with two valves per cylinder activated by pushrods from a central camshaft. However, that's where any similarity to the original Hemi ends. Every part and component in a modern Top Fuel dragster

ABOVE The perfect view on launch: inlet butterflies on the injector hat wide open at full throttle with nitro flames bursting from the headers. *(Dom Romney)*

RIGHT A huge supercharger sits between the cylinder heads, and on top of that is a massive carbon fibre injector hat. *(Mark Skinner)*

BELOW The large engine block sits centrally with a massive cylinder head each side. *(Mark Skinner)*

engine is specially built for purpose. The engine is mounted solid to the chassis rails by motor plates, one at the front made of T6 aluminium and one at the rear made from chromoly and sandwiched between the rear of the block and the titanium clutch can. It's mechanically fuel-injected and supercharged by a Roots-type supercharger, or 'blower' as it's more commonly known in the drag racing world. Turbochargers and/or centrifugal superchargers are prohibited. A carbon fibre fuel injector hat is then mounted on top of the blower.

The regulations

Founded in 1951, the NHRA (National Hot Rod Association) governs the sport of drag racing in the USA as well as hosting championship races across North America. Each year it produces a rule book by which all new and existing vehicles must abide. European Drag Racing comes under the FIA banner, and this means that there are slight variations in rules, but by and large they remain very close. New regulations are constantly being introduced by the NHRA, with European teams adopting these changes around one year later. For the American teams, these updates are often much easier to implement due to their huge race budgets, whereas European teams with smaller budgets can often find it difficult to keep up with such upgrades. That said, the modern FIA European Top Fuel dragster won't be far behind its American cousin.

Engine design and build

In the world of Formula 1 each team will have a contract with an engine supplier, *eg* McLaren–Mercedes. When designing and building their car for the coming season, the engineers from the engine manufacturer will work very closely with the team's designers during the design process.

However, Top Fuel drag racing teams in Europe don't have this kind of relationship with an engine manufacturer, although they may well have a preferred supplier that they'll look to buy either a block or heads etc from, and will then build this up with their own choice of parts. Throughout the Top Fuel drag racing class the engines are built in-house by the teams themselves.

Engine building will vary for each team, but all parts are bought from American

The following engine regulations are those stipulated by the NHRA:
- The engine must be a 90° (the angle between cylinder banks) V8.
- This must use a single camshaft, with no overhead cams permitted.
- The cubic inch displacement of the engine must be a maximum of 500 and a minimum of 490.
- Cylinder bore centre spacing must be a maximum of 4.800in.
- Maximum cam centreline must be 5.400in.
- There must be a maximum of two valves per cylinder.
- Only one cylinder head design is acceptable: the intake valve angle must be 35°, plus or minus 1°. The exhaust valve angle must be 21°, plus or minus 1°.
- The engine block must be machined from forged aluminium.

manufacturers, so that teams are often in the hands of shipping agents in order to complete their build processes.

The biggest difference between Top Fuel drag racing and other motorsports is the total engine rebuild that's required between runs.

Cylinder block

The cylinder block is machined from a piece of forged aluminium. Cast-aluminium blocks have been hugely popular with racers

BELOW The biggest difference between Top Fuel drag racing and other motorsports is the total engine rebuild that's required between runs.
(Mark Skinner)

for decades, but forged blocks are much stronger although slightly heavier as the material is denser. As there are no water passages in the block, cooling is provided by the oil and the huge amount of fuel that goes through a Top Fuel motor during a run. Each cylinder has a ductile cast-iron liner inserted, specially made using a centrifugal casting process. These liners are often replaced between runs if need be.

RIGHT AND BELOW There are no water passages in the block – cooling is provided by the oil and the huge amount of fuel that goes through a Top Fuel motor during a run. *(Mark Skinner)*

ABOVE AND BELOW Each cylinder has a ductile cast-iron liner inserted, specially made using a centrifugal casting process. These liners are often replaced between runs if need be. *(Mark Skinner)*

Cylinder heads

The cylinder heads have a hemispherical combustion chamber and are machined from billet aluminium.

The intake valves are made from titanium and are 2.45in (62.2mm) in diameter. The maximum diameter allowed is 2.70in.

The exhaust valves are manufactured from solid Inconel – a combination of austenitic nickel-chromium-based superalloys that tends to be used in high temperature applications (and thus perfect for Top Fuel engine applications) – and are usually 1.925in (48.9mm) in diameter, the maximum diameter allowed being 2in. The valve seats are made from ductile iron. The cylinder heads are secured to the block by 17 nuts on aircraft-rated steel studs.

ABOVE The cylinder heads have a hemispherical combustion chamber and are machined from billet aluminium. *(Mark Skinner)*

LEFT The intake valves are made from titanium and are 2.45in (62.2mm) in diameter. The maximum diameter allowed is 2.70in. *(Mark Skinner)*

BELOW LEFT AND RIGHT Valves and springs in situ in the cylinder head. *(Mark Skinner)*

LEFT AND BELOW The cylinder heads are secured to the block by 17 nuts on aircraft-rated steel studs. *(Mark Skinner)*

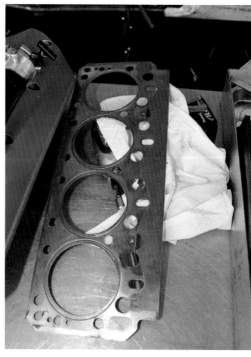

Between the head and the block is a solid copper head gasket, and each cylinder head also has four stainless steel O-rings that are fitted into a groove that's machined in the cylinder head and runs round each combustion chamber to aid sealing. These are needed to cope with the massive cylinder pressures that are generated within a supercharged nitro-burning engine.

Crankshaft

The crankshaft weighs around 79lb and is made from billet steel. It has five main bearings. Although incredibly strong, teams will normally limit the number of runs to around 20 (five miles) on each crankshaft to reduce the risk of failure. The main crank journal is usually 2¾in.

Bearings

All bearings in the crankshaft assembly are conventional half-shell bearings. The big end bearings are replaced after each pass. The main bearings are checked after each run and replaced as required.

Pistons and connecting rods

Forged aluminium pistons are used, combining high strength with light weight. They're

ABOVE AND RIGHT All bearings are conventional half-shell types. The big end bearings are replaced after each pass. The main bearings are checked after each run and replaced as required. *(Mark Skinner)*

mounted to the connecting rod with 1.156 x 3.300in steel gudgeon pins. These are secured by aluminium buttons that are located in each side of the piston and held in place by one of three piston rings.

The piston is also anodised and Teflon-coated to prevent damage during high-temperature operation. The top ring provides a good seal during combustion but a second ring must be used to prevent oil from entering

RIGHT Forged aluminium pistons are used, combining high strength with light weight. The piston is anodised and Teflon-coated to prevent damage during high-temperature operation.
(Mark Skinner)

LEFT The connecting rods are also manufactured from forged aluminium and have a life span of five miles or 20 passes.
(Mark Skinner)

ABOVE Pistons in their liners seated in the block. *(Mark Skinner)*

RIGHT A box of used liners and pistons. These will often be sold as souvenirs to race fans. *(Mark Skinner)*

RIGHT AND BELOW All Top Fuel engines use mechanical roller lifters that move the pushrods into the steel rockers that open the valves. The rocker arms are mounted on a pair of titanium shafts, one for inlet and the other for exhaust rockers. *(Mark Skinner)*

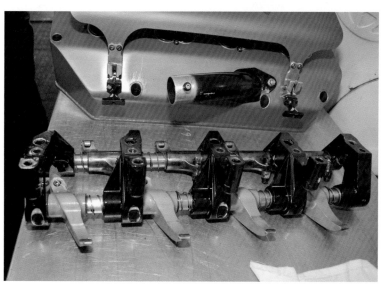

the combustion chamber. The third ring is an oil scraper ring whose function is helped by the second ring. The connecting rods are also manufactured from forged aluminium and have a life span of five miles or 20 passes.

Camshaft

The camshaft runs in five oil pressure lubricated bearing shells. It's made of billet steel and is driven by steel gears on the front of the engine. All Top Fuel engines use mechanical roller lifters that move the pushrods into the steel rockers that open the valves. The intake and exhaust rockers are of roller type.

The rocker arms are mounted on a pair of titanium shafts, one for inlet and the other for exhaust rockers. The valve springs are triple springs and are made of titanium and held in place by titanium retainers and steel collets.

Flywheel

The flywheel smoothes the power delivery to the rear wheels by using a large rotating mass to damp the pulses of each cylinder. It's made of titanium and is located on to the rear of the crankshaft by two dowels and then held in place by eight ½in diameter bolts. In the centre of the flywheel is a pilot bearing in which the nose of the input shaft runs. There's no ring

ABOVE **The triple valve springs are made of titanium.** *(Mark Skinner)*

ABOVE **The core of the ignition system is two massive 44A magnetos sending out 1,200 milliamps of current.** *(Mark Skinner)*

BELOW **The mags are easily serviceable between runs.**

(Mark Skinner)

gear on the flywheel as in a conventional vehicle because a Top Fuel dragster doesn't have an on-board starter motor.

The five-disc clutch pack is held in place against the flywheel by the titanium clutch cover or pressure plate. This whole flywheel/ clutch assembly is contained within the titanium bellhousing, or clutch can as it's more commonly known in drag racing.

Rules state that the titanium clutch can must meet SFI Spec 6.2. The maximum depth allowed for this can is 9.4in. Aluminium flywheels are not permitted.

Ignition and timing

The core of the ignition system is two massive 44A magnetos sending out 1,200 milliamps of current. These are driven off a gear on the front end of the engine's camshaft.

From the bottom of the magneto a hexagonal shaft runs down through the engine block and into the oil pump, providing oil pump drive. This large amount of spark is needed due to the amount of fuel and air injected into each cylinder. Ignition timing is normally between 52°–65° before top dead centre depending on track conditions. This is much more advanced than would be used in a petrol engine, as nitro burns slower. Each cylinder has two spark

plugs that are changed after every pass.

At 0.8 of a second into a run, depending on track conditions the timing is typically retarded by 14° for 0.5 of a second (again this time is dependent on track conditions). This helps the car to settle after the launch and allows the tyres time to reach their correct shape. The ignition system limits the engine speed to 8,400rpm. The ignition system provides an initial 50,000V and 1.2A. The long-duration spark (up to 26°) provides energy of 950

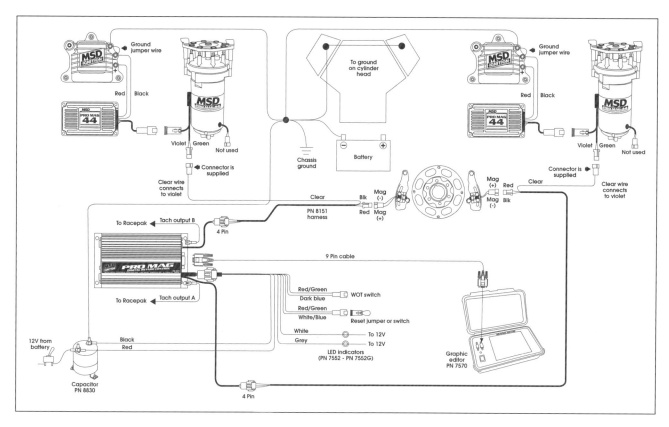

Labels within diagram:
Ground jumper wire

MSD IGNITION

Red   Black

MSD PRO MAG 44

Violet Green   Not used

Clear wire connects to violet

Connector is supplied

To ground on cylinder head

Chassis ground

Battery

Ground jumper wire

MSD IGNITION

Red   Black

MSD PRO MAG 44

Violet Green   Not used

Connector is supplied

Clear wire connects to violet

Clear

Blk   Mag (-)
Red   Mag (+)

PN 8151 harness

Mag (+)
Mag (-)

Red
Blk

Clear

To Racepak ← Tach output B

4 Pin

PRO MAG DIGITAL TIMING CONTROL

9 Pin cable

To Racepak ← Tach output A

Red/Green
Dark blue   WOT switch

Red/Green
White/Blue   Reset jumper or switch

White   To 12V
Grey   To 12V

LED indicators
(PN 7552 – PN 7552G)

Graphic editor
PN 7570

12V from battery

Black
Red

Capacitor
PN 8830

4 Pin

millijoules. The plugs are placed in such a way that they're cooled by the incoming charge. The ignition system isn't allowed to respond to real-time information (ie there are no computer-based spark lead adjustments), so instead a time-based advance/retard system is used.

Fuel system

Along with the clutch set-up the fuel system is key to successful performance in a Top Fuel dragster. Once it was discovered that you could pump large amounts of nitro into an engine, the next job was to increase fuel flow.

Mounted on the front of the engine is a large, four-gear fuel pump that produces a pressure of 500–600psi. Modern Top Fuel cars have a flow rate of up to 100 gallons per minute. Braided lines connect the pump to a barrel valve mounted on the injector. This valve is connected to the injector's butterflies by a hexagonal linkage, with a small rose joint at either end. Fuel is injected into the engine by at least (depending on tuner) 36 separate injectors: 16 are hidden under the rocker boxes and screw into the inlet port (these spray directly on to the inlet valve); there are usually eight in the inlet manifold, one in each inlet tract; and a further 12 are mounted at the bottom of the injector hat – these spray directly into the top of the supercharger.

When a Top Fuel car is idling it will still use around 3 gallons of nitro a minute. From start-up to burnout and staging between 5–7 gallons will be consumed, and during a run a Top Fuel dragster will consume around 1½ gallons of fuel per second. In summary, from fire-up to turning off at the top end the car will have consumed around 14 gallons of fuel!

Superchargers

TF dragsters are restricted to a Roots-type supercharger, in Top Fuel racing circles known simply as a 'blower'. The Roots name comes from American inventors and brothers Philander and Francis Roots, who founded the Roots Blower Company in Indiana and first patented their design in 1860. At this time it was used as an air pump for various industrial applications. It was Gottlieb Daimler who first introduced the design to the automotive world in 1900, when he included a Roots-type supercharger in a patented engine design. Roots blowers can also be found referred to as 'air blowers' or 'positive displacement' blowers.

The twisted lobes of the supercharger are driven by a large Kevlar blower belt on the front. This is driven off the crankshaft and can spin at up to 12,000rpm. These belts are of a special Poly Chain toothed construction. They're 75mm wide, with the modern design providing a 14mm pitch – the distance between belt teeth.

The engine crankshaft will go from idle (2,300rpm) to around 8,200rpm, and should the dragster lose traction and the driver have to come on and off the throttle it could drop back down to around 5,000rpm; the inertial load of the blower wants to keep accelerating despite the drop in engine rpm. Effectively the two are now working against each other, causing a change in belt tension, often resulting in breakages.

A belt is expected to last for four runs, but some teams opt for a more frequent change. When Carter and Andersen Racing suffered a series of breaks during the 2008 season they opted to change the belt on every single pass.

The modern Top Fuel blower is a derivative of the General Motors 6-71 blower, originally designed for their two-stroke diesel engines. This was then adapted for drag racing use in the '60s. The 6-71 name was derived from its size, making reference to the GM diesel motor having six cylinders with 71in^3 per cylinder. Today's Top

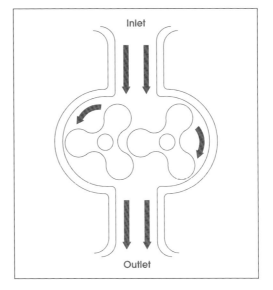

ABOVE The supercharger on a Top Fuel dragster is restricted to a Roots-type supercharger, in Top Fuel drag racing circles known simply as a 'blower'. *(Mark Skinner)*

LEFT The basic principle of a Roots-type blower. It was Gottlieb Daimler who first introduced this design to the automotive world in 1900. *(Illustration by 3tc)*

LEFT Here the internal, twisted lobes of the blower are clearly visible. *(Mark Skinner)*

RIGHT These lobes are driven by a large Kevlar blower belt on the front. This is driven off the crankshaft and can spin at up to 12,000rpm.
(Mark Skinner)

RIGHT A belt is expected to last for four runs, but some teams opt for a more frequent change. They can often break on a run as a result of sudden change in engine rpm.
(Mark Skinner)

RIGHT An intake manifold sits on top of the blower. A burst plate must be incorporated, designed to open at around 200psi and prevent huge pressure build-up causing a full supercharger explosion.
(Mark Skinner)

Fuel blowers mustn't exceed 14-71, representing a sizeable increase from the original design.

The 14-71 blower must have a maximum case length of 22¼in and a maximum width of 11¼in. The case is required to be one-piece, with removable front and rear bearing end plates. Rotors are limited to a maximum length of 19in, with a maximum diameter of 5.840in. The top opening mustn't exceed 11.750in long by 4.600in in width. Any spacers between the top of the blower case and the injector hat mustn't exceed 2½in and must be constructed from aluminium or composite materials.

Internally two three-bladed helical rotors are meshed together like two three-toothed gears. These are synchronised by two external gears to prevent them coming into contact with each other. As they spin they compress the air that's fed into the cylinders. By changing pulley sizes the crew chief can increase the amount of boost produced by the supercharger through increased speed. This speed increase over one-to-one is called overdrive, with a typical overdrive being around 40%. At maximum pressure it takes around 900–1,000hp just to drive the supercharger. An intake manifold burst plate must be incorporated, designed to open at around 200psi and prevent huge pressure build-up causing a full supercharger explosion.

The modern superchargers are mounted offset to the rear. This provides better fuel and air distribution into the cylinders.

RIGHT As well as the mandatory burst plate a secured Kevlar-style blanket or 'blower bag' around the supercharger assembly is required, to contain the blower and its components in the event of an explosion. *(Mark Skinner)*

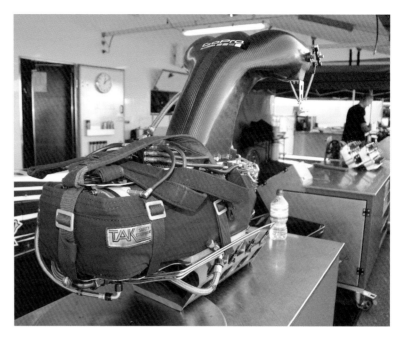

As well as the mandatory burst plate mounted in the inlet manifold a secured Kevlar-style blanket or 'blower bag' around the supercharger assembly is required, to contain the blower and its components in the event of a blower explosion. The bag and its restraint straps must be fully flame-resistant. The blower bag is held in place by four straps fixed to brackets that are bolted on to the exhaust header studs.

Fuel injector hat

A large fuel injector hat sits on top of the blower and must have a maximum air inlet opening of 65in². The maximum height accepted from the crankshaft centreline to the top of the hat is 46in. Looking at the hat from the front the most popular configuration is three large 'butterfly' openings controlled by a very heavy-duty

LEFT The blower will be serviced in the pit between runs. *(Mark Skinner)*

BELOW The maximum height accepted from the crankshaft centreline to the top of the hat is 46in. *(Illustrations by 3tc)*

BELOW A large fuel injector hat sits on top of the blower and must have a maximum air inlet opening of 65in². *(Gary Cottingham)*

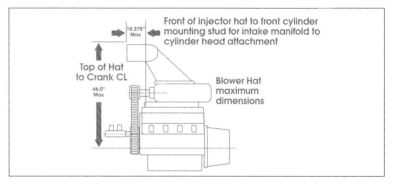

Front of injector hat to front cylinder mounting stud for intake manifold to cylinder head attachment

10.375" Max

Top of Hat to Crank CL

46.0" Max

Blower Hat maximum dimensions

LEFT The most popular injector hat configuration consists of three large 'butterfly' openings that are controlled by a very heavy-duty throttle cable. *(Mark Skinner)*

Nitromethane is one of a group of chemicals known as nitroalkanes, which consist of an alkane molecule, such as methane, ethane or propane, in which one of the hydrogen atoms has been replaced by a nitro group (-NO2). Nitromethane is used in a number of products, including fuels, explosives, solvents, preservatives and pharmaceuticals. Angus Chemical's nitromethane manufacturing process results in the joint production of four nitroalkanes, of which nitromethane has the highest value.

Standard nitromethane (CH_3NO_2) becomes di-nitromethane when exposed to UV (ultra violet rays), which is more entertaining to run. All commercially available nitromethane is never available at 100%. It's typically cut (reduced in concentration) by approximately 2% or so with benzene or other agents. Besides, 100% won't light very well without being cut with something. Back in the old days, some folks were indeed getting hold of *real* 100% (from other than normal suppliers) and cut the load by 2% with spectrophotometric benzene (not your normal get-it-anywhere benzene).

Purple nitro

Potassium permanganate (KMnO4) can be mixed and, although a slurry, can be burned with either methanol, nitromethane or nitropropane. Also one can add methyl purple (no gain, just fun colouring), methyl orange, or methyl blue. You can even add oil of wintergreen if you wish.

Like an atomic device, the separate components of a fission-fusion device are relatively benign, but when a special set of artificial conditions is created it'll produce a dramatic result. Nitromethane is the atomic equivalent of uranium U235 (raw uranium is about 99.3% U238 and about 0.7% U235, which is the stuff that goes bang and the reason for all the refining). Getting it to burn is a major problem: it needs lots of heat. But once the correct temperature is achieved, it'll give more energy than most people can use.

A match won't light nitromethane. Dropped into a pool of nitro spillage on the floor a match will sizzle and extinguish, just as if it had fallen in a pool of tap water. But take a hammer and hit the pool, and it'll explode. The small amount of fuel caught between the hammer face and the concrete floor will become unstable and cause a spontaneous fire that occurs quickly enough to be labelled an explosion. The tiny bit of lit fuel is hot enough to set off the rest. And the bigger the pool, the bigger the explosion. Enough nitro and the result will be a good-sized crater in the cement floor.

Joe Fette, a former vice president and general manager of Angus Chemical, worked intimately with the nitromethane departments, and remembers when the discovery was made. 'The condition first came about by accident,' says Fette. 'Luckily, it was an accident where nobody was killed. But nitromethane used to be shipped in tank cars before this condition was known. Two separate accidents within a year of each other stopped that. The tank cars exploded, leaving holes 800ft wide and 300ft deep. Luckily, these were out in unpopulated areas. What happened is that the fuel was compressed when it slammed into the other car (as the train crashed). There were also rumours of power lines being around, although that was never proven.

'Regardless of an external spark, the impact had sufficient force to begin the reaction that would ignite the explosive. The liquid, trapped inside the tanks, had nowhere to go and compressed itself. Under those circumstances it detonated by itself – at least in the corner of the container that suffered the largest degree of compression. With the initial explosion, extreme heat – the second factor that contributes to nitromethane's instability – was already building up. With nowhere to go the heat spread through the compressed fuel in the tanker, setting the entire railroad car on fire before the structure had been punctured. The result was an explosion that changed the land's geography.'

Chinese nitro is still being made in China at a specially constructed plant. It's imported to the US by the Wego Chemical Company in New York. It's made by a different process than Angus (now Dow Chemical as of two to three years ago) nitro. A test was done on the three nitro products that were available in 1996 and they found the Chinese nitro to be more pure than the Angus nitro, and much more pure than the product that VP was selling at the time. Those results may not hold up now, but they were accurate at the time the products were tested.

Nitromethane CH_3NO_2 CAS Reg No 75-52-5 EINECS No 200-87-66

Nitromethane, if not properly handled, stored or used, can be dangerous and can detonate. Nitromethane should only be handled, stored or used by trained personnel who fully understand nitromethane properties and have read and understand the appropriate data sheet.

Nitromethane (NM) is a versatile chemical with a wide variety of industrial applications. It's used as a stabiliser for halogenated hydrocarbons, as a component of special fuels for internal combustion engines, as a solvent for polymers in coating, and as a synthesis of many useful chemicals such as chloropicrin and tris (hydroxymethyl) aminomethane.

Nitromethane was first prepared in 1872 by Adolf Wilhelm Kolbe, and for many years was considered to be a very stable compound. It wasn't until 1938 that scientist D.S. McKittrick and his co-workers reported that nitromethane could be detonated under conditions of strong confinement.

The characteristics of nitromethane have been studied by agencies such as the US Army Chemical Corps and the California Institute of Technology. These studies have identified three conditions under which nitromethane can be detonated:

- A very severe shock, in excess of that provided by a No8 blasting cap.
- Severe and very rapid compression under adiabatic conditions.
- Liquid nitromethane can be detonated when heated under confinement to near its critical temperature.

Sensitisation of nitromethane will increase the ease of initiation of detonation by all of these mechanisms. Nitromethane is sensitised by the addition of a few per cent of certain compounds, particularly amines, or by elevated temperatures.

Used by kind permission of www.wdifl.com

throttle cable. At full throttle these butterflies will be fully open, allowing maximum air intake. During the pre-run burnout procedure a throttle stop is fitted to the cable to limit the amount of throttle travel applied. This is then removed by a crew member prior to the car moving into stage, ready to run.

The fuel

As you move up through the various classes within drag racing, the fuel used shifts from regular pump gasoline, to methanol, to the pinnacle – nitromethane, or nitro, produced by the nitration of propane, the end result being CH_3NO_2.

In a Top Fuel dragster nitro is mixed with racing methanol, and the amount of nitro allowed to be used is limited by the NHRA to a maximum of 90%, with a lesser mix also being permitted.

ABOVE AND ABOVE RIGHT As the car is warmed up in the pit area a heavy, yellow cloud will form. Without a mask such as those worn by the crew and driver, the mix is choking and acts like tear gas. *(Gary Cottingham)*

Nitro has a much lower energy density than the other fuels: nitro = 11.2MJ/kg (megajoules per kilogram), gasoline = 44MJ/kg, and methanol = 22.7MJ/kg. Burning nitro in an engine can produce up to 2.3 times more power than an engine running on gasoline. This is because an engine must admit air in order to generate force. To burn one kilogram of gasoline 14.7kg of air is required, compared to nitro where only 1.7kg is required. This means that compared to gasoline, you can pump about eight times more nitro into a cylinder and still get complete combustion.

Nitro also has a high latent heat of vaporisation. This means that it can absorb high engine heat as it vaporises, thus offering invaluable cooling properties.

Overall power output can be increased by using very rich air/fuel mixtures. This also helps prevent pre-ignition, something that's often a problem when running on nitro.

Due to their slow burn rate, very rich fuel mixtures are often not fully ignited, and therefore the unburnt nitro can escape from the exhaust headers and ignite on contact with atmospheric oxygen. This is often seen burning with characteristic yellow flames from the headers. After sufficient fuel has been combusted to consume all the available oxygen, nitro can still combust in the absence of atmospheric oxygen, thus producing hydrogen. This can be seen burning from the headers at night as white flame.

Lubrication system

A Top Fuel dragster has a wet aluminium sump that contains 16 litres of oil. The Carter Motorsport car uses 70-weight Lucas mineral oil. In colder temperatures 50w or 60w is sometimes used. Oil is heated before being put into the engine.

The aluminium pan mustn't extend forward of the lower blower pulley nor rearwards past the crossmember under the axle pinion flange. The pans should either be a one-piece unit or designed in such a way that, when constructed,

RIGHT A Top Fuel dragster has a wet aluminium sump that contains 16 litres of oil. *(Mark Skinner)*

FAR RIGHT Here the sump is drained after a run. *(Mark Skinner)*

ABOVE **The pan will be completely removed, inspected and cleaned between runs.** *(Mark Skinner)*

ABOVE **A Top Fuel dragster engine has eight individual exhaust pipes sitting in banks of four on each side of the engine.** *(Gary Cottingham)*

BELOW AND BOTTOM **The exhausts on each side of the engine are often referred to as headers. Here you can see how they're braced together, as well as the sensors used for data logging.** *(Mark Skinner)*

they form a sealed unit. The bulkheads of the pan must be at least 4in high, and the pan width mustn't be wider than the outside edge of the bottom frame rails.

All retention devices (commonly called 'diapers' in drag racing) must contain a non-flammable, oil-absorbent liner.

The oil pump pressure varies from around 240psi on start-up to somewhere between 160–170psi during a pass, but these figures will vary between teams and according to the type of oil pump used.

Exhaust

A Top Fuel dragster engine has eight individual exhaust pipes sitting in banks of four on each side of the engine. These are referred to as 'headers'.

The exhaust gases are forced upwards and back from the headers; this provides additional downforce for increased traction. Each pipe is 2¾in in diameter, 18in in length, made of steel, and is fitted with a thermocoupler to measure exhaust temperature. This is around 500°F (260°C) at idle and 1,796°F (980°C) at the end of a run.

The huge flames that can be seen extending from the headers on a run, especially on a night run, are one of the most impressive sights in motorsport.

HEADER FLAMES: THE EYE, THE CAMERA

Some folks think nitro header flames are just hot exhaust gas, but this isn't true. The exhaust gas temperatures aren't nearly hot enough to make them incandescent. What we see as header flames is real fire, the continuing combustion of unburned cylinder charge after it's pushed out of the engine. It's *combustion* flame. The combustion continues and even accelerates once the exhaust charge starts expanding and dissipating into the atmosphere, where it encounters additional oxygen to help it along.

So a header flame actually has two stages: the first at the exit of the header pipe, then a second as it expands into the atmosphere. The first stage can be thought of as a 'pulse' having a frequency and duration defined by

the mechanics of the engine. The second stage is a flame front whose size and duration is determined by combustion dynamics.

With respect to the first stage, the 'frequency' that flame is going to appear at each header pipe is, of course, a direct function of engine rpm. It's going to appear at every exhaust stroke, or once every other engine revolution – 1,200 times a minute at a 'nominal' 2,400rpm idle – 4,200 times a minute at a 'nominal' 8,400rpm maximum engine speed. Expressed in terms of Hz (cycles per second), these figures correspond to 20Hz and 70Hz. (The 'nominal' figures are for illustration purposes, and the reason I translate this as Hz will be apparent later.)

Still with respect to the first stage, the

BELOW Header flames are a spectacular sight in Top Fuel drag racing. They're often referred to as 'bunny ears'.
(Andy Carter Collection)

'duration' of the flame pulse at the header tube exit is also a mechanical engine function. It corresponds (more or less) to the length of time the exhaust valve is open (with some variables in flow dynamics interfering to make this an approximation). Let's arbitrarily say it's one third of the 720° cycle. That makes it two-thirds the duration of a single engine revolution. So at idle that works out to 1/60th of a second (.0166 seconds), while at 8,400rpm it's 1/210th of a second (.0047 seconds).

Remember that with this simplification the duration of each flow pulse is followed by a duration twice as long during which there *is no* flow. These durations, relative to camera shutter speeds, are significant, as will be seen later.

Moving on to the second stage, we have to consider how long it takes for the unburnt fuel in the exhaust pulse to finish burning. This will be hugely variable and dependent on many operational factors, but suffice to say that at racing rpm it's *way* longer than the duration of the exhaust pulse itself, and more on the order of a tenth of a second or even longer. In effect, then, as engine speed increases we have more and more fresh pulses of exhaust adding to the stream of still-burning mixture in the expansion area further away from the pipe. Net result: a 'continuous flame' area at some distance outboard.

Now on to how the human eye and cameras perceive this.

Human vision is affected by the phenomenon of 'latency' that relates to the response time of our neuroreceptors. In practical terms, we can respond to changes in light intensity only so fast, and the higher the frequency and longer the duration of the light stimulus, the more uniform it appears. Light pulses at 20Hz appear to flicker. At 70Hz they appear continuous. Examples might be how a strobe light looks as you crank up the frequency (the appearance of the illumination from your timing light with the engine at idle versus high speed), or the 'flicker' on a computer monitor with too low a 'refresh' rate compared to the smoothness of one that is optimum (72Hz or higher). Motion pictures rely upon this phenomenon to make sequential images presented at 30Hz appear continuous,

with only moderate flicker. (They do call 'em 'the flicks' after all!) From the above figures concerning header flame frequency, you can appreciate why individual pulses at the pipe tips are generally discernable at idle or off-idle rpm but will appear to be continuous streams in the racing rpm range.

Camera film and electronic CCDs don't exhibit latency (or at least very little), and with adjustable shutter speeds are able to record events that occur too quickly for human eye response. From the above figures on exhaust pulse frequencies, it's apparent how selection of shutter speed can affect how many cylinders appear to be firing at a given engine speed. The slower the shutter, the more likely multiple cylinders will be caught 'in the act'. The faster the shutter, the more likelihood only one or two will exhibit flame at the pipe's tip. You can do the math and see precisely what I mean. Similarly, as far as the 'continuous flame area' is concerned, the slower the shutter the larger the continuous flame area will likely appear to be, and the faster the shutter the more definition it's likely to have.

Now for the $64 question about ESPN super slow-mo shots and the odd header flame patterns revealed, especially during tyre-shake. I can't be sure without knowing more specifics about the camera frame rate and shutter speeds, but the possibility exists that if the shutter speed is 'in synch' or 'in phase' with engine speed, you could get a strobe-like effect that catches the same cylinder several times in succession while ignoring others, creating an artefact appearance when displayed as a motion picture. Frankly, though, I doubt that's the case. I more suspect you're seeing a real phenomenon – basically erratic cylinder firing due to the wildly fluctuating engine loads and component torsional response due to traction variation. Shutter speed is fast enough to catch individual cylinders in the act of misbehaving, which they may only do for a few revs. At least that's my bet. All this would be missed at slower (normal) shutter speeds, which would tend to homogenise everything together much as our eyesight would.

Vic Cooke
(used by kind permission of www.wdifl.com)

ABOVE The throttle pedal is connected to the injector butterflies by a heavy-duty cable. *(Mark Skinner)*

ABOVE RIGHT The driver's throttle pedal is linked to a cable that runs along the side of the chassis rail, up to the injector hat. *(Mark Skinner)*

RIGHT A throttle stop is used to prevent full throttle being applied during the burnout. *(Dom Romney)*

RIGHT Starting the motor is done by crew members by means of a large starter motor attached to the top pulley on the front of the blower. *(Mark Skinner)*

Throttle control

The throttle is a fully manual system. The throttle pedal is connected to the injector butterflies by a heavy-duty Bowden cable that runs from the driver's foot pedal and along the side of the chassis rail, secured by cable ties, and, once past the driver's seat, up to the injector hat.

Starting system

There's no driver-operated starter on a Top Fuel dragster. Starting the motor is done by crew members externally. A large starter motor is attached to the top pulley on the front of the blower. This has its own button to activate itself. As one crew member operates the hand-held starter motor, another squirts petrol directly into the injector hat. As this is happening, another crew member is pulling the kill leads off the coils, allowing the ignition to become live. Once the motor has fired on petrol, the crew member who pulled the kill leads will turn on the fuel pump, allowing the flow of nitro into the engine.

The starter motor runs off its own external battery supply, usually 36V.

Transmission

When you've got so much horsepower under the throttle pedal, the biggest challenge to a Top Fuel dragster crew chief is how to make sure you apply the power to the track correctly. These cars don't use a transmission, so how do you get the available power to the rear wheels? You use a clutch; but it's not perhaps anything you may be familiar with. If you were to attend a race you may hear a commentator, driver or crew member comment on clutch settings by using phrases like 'We had too much clutch'. This would usually result in violent tyre shake or a loss of traction from the rear tyres. 'Too little clutch' can often result in tyre shake too, or a soft run with the car not getting up on the rear tyres as it should. Simply put, with the amount of power available you can't possibly put it to the ground in one hit. There has to be a way of applying the power progressively during the course of a run, allowing the car to launch from standing and then apply 100% of the available power. As one racer put it: 'In every class, the race is won or lost in the bellhousing.'

ABOVE The clutch pack. The cylindrical titanium rods known as stands are also shown. *(Mark Skinner)*

I could write a book of its own about the Top Fuel clutch, but the following should explain sufficiently how this complicated system works.

The clutch consists of a five- or six-disc clutch pack, depending on the crew chief's preference. These are made of sintered iron, with steel floaters (an American term that describes a shaped piece of steel that sits between two clutch plates in a clutch assembly) that create a pack, with one side of the pack attached to the flywheel of the engine. The pack would be as follows: flywheel – clutch plate – floater – clutch plate – floater – clutch plate – floater – clutch plate – floater – clutch plate – pressure plate.

The clutch pack operates with a varying degree of slippage throughout a run, until it locks up around 660ft or 3.1 seconds into

LEFT The levers that cause the clamping force are tuned by their pivot angle, weight and the order in which they're allowed to move outwards. *(Mark Skinner)*

RIGHT Clutch discs ready to be included in the pack assembly, the assembly having been removed from the pack after a run and cleaned. *(Mark Skinner)*

BELOW The clutch pack is housed in a titanium bellhousing. *(Mark Skinner)*

the run. The earlier you can do this the faster you go. The amount of slippage and point of lock-up is determined by the crew chief, and this is where they really earn their money. Slippage time and full lock-up time is dictated by the engine tuner, weather conditions, track conditions and who you're racing against.

The clutch is activated by the rpm of the engine and is basically a massive centrifugal clutch. There are a number of 'stands', which drive the floaters and levers. Clutch stands are part of the clutch assembly. They're inch-diameter cylindrical titanium rods that connect to the flywheel at a 90° angle. The clutch floaters attach to these stands; they're of varying thicknesses and are replaced after every run but can be serviced and reused for up to four runs. The levers deliver the clamping force and are tuned by their pivot angle, weight, and the order in which they're allowed to move out. All levers can be adjusted by the crew chief.

As the clutch spins its fingers are forced outwards, compressing the clutch and allowing more power to be applied to the rear wheels.

Aside from the fingers, there's also a series of timers – pneumatic or electronic – that control a release bearing that's attached to the clutch cannon. At points during the run this moves backwards at pre-determined points, allowing the fingers to come out, which in turn allows the clutch to progressively lock up.

Clutch cannon

The clutch cannon is mounted between the titanium bellhousing that houses the clutch and the reverser. It's a hydraulically operated device that's connected to the release bearing inside the bellhousing.

When the clutch cannon is set before a run, it pushes the release bearing up against the levers on the clutch pressure plate. When the driver starts the run and pushes the accelerator to the floor, this operates a switch that starts the clutch timer operation. The cannon then

LEFT The bellhousing is one of a number of parts that must be tested and approved at the start of a new season by the SFI. *(Courtesy Tog, Eurodragster.com)*

moves away from the fingers, allowing them to come out and lock up the clutch.

Typically, a clutch will be set up to engage enough to launch the car off the line at around 8,000rpm. Adding weight to the fingers means that the clutch will engage at lower rpm, whereas lightening them will allow the motor to rev higher before engaging. The timers are then activated by a microswitch under the throttle pedal. Hit the throttle and the timers will start to run with the aim of a fully locked-up clutch by around the one-eighth mile mark. It's make or break point when all the power is applied. If you don't go up in smoke at this point then you're on your way to a good run.

The amount of wear on a Top Fuel clutch is anywhere between 110–125 thousandths, with a visible cloud of clutch dust seen behind the car on a run. This occurs during the controlled slip stage of the run prior to lock-up. A clutch disc will only make two runs in Europe before being scrapped, but in the US a disc will be lucky to make more than one appearance in a pack.

As you can imagine, the heat generated from the clutch assembly is immense and the clutch

LEFT The clutch cannon is a hydraulically operated device that's connected to the release bearing inside the bellhousing. During a run the cannon moves away from the clutch fingers, allowing them to come out and lock up the clutch. *(Mark Skinner)*

ABOVE Between the clutch and rear axle is the reverser. Although not a transmission the reverser has a set of planetary gears which, when engaged, reverse the output to the rear axle.
(Mark Skinner)

man on the crew will wear asbestos gloves as he pulls the unit apart after a run. The heat generated has been known to weld the discs and floaters together!

Between the clutch and rear axle is the reverser. Although not a transmission the reverser has a set of planetary gears which, when engaged, reverse the output to the rear axle. This enables the car to reverse back after it's performed the burnout. Engaging reverse is done by a cable-operated lever in the driver's cockpit. All reverser units are required to be covered by a one-piece ballistic Kevlar blanket. This blanket must be SFI-approved.

The clutch on a run

So just how much use does the clutch pedal have during a run? When the engine is fired up, prior to a run the driver will have his foot on the clutch pedal fully depressed and the handbrake hard on. Once motioned forward by a crew member the driver can then let the clutch out so that the car can move forward, but at this point it's slipping significantly.

As the driver performs the burnout the primary levers engage the clutch and the tyres spin. When you come off the throttle pedal the clutch goes back into slip mode, but it's also dragging until you stop with the clutch pedal fully depressed to engage reverse. Let the pedal out again and the car will start to back up. Once rolling, put the pedal in again and coast back to the start line. This limits the amount of heat

build-up in the clutch before the run. You move the car into stage by pushing in the clutch, engaging forward again, letting the pedal out and moving forward slowly towards pre-stage. Once in pre-stage depress the clutch and wait for your opponent to reach the same point. At this point the driver will pull the fuel pump on full and grab the handbrake, then let out the clutch completely. The car will obviously pull against the brake, but you work the brakes to pull you into full stage. At this point the clutch pedal's work is done and it's all about the right foot. It's worth mentioning that during the run the clutch pedal will be moving back upwards by itself, as it's connected to the cannon by a rod. Therefore the driver must make sure that his foot is clear of the pedal as this movement occurs.

Data logging

Knowing how important the clutch set-up is and how hard it is to get this right, it's difficult to believe that for years the clutch was set without the aid of a data logger. The set-up was down to the crew chief's knowledge or the driver's feel within the car, as well as their observations and, of course, the wear on the clutch. This trial and error process is now avoided through a data logger.

Computer control isn't allowed anywhere on dragsters or Funny Cars, but sensored logging is permitted. Items such as clutch temperature, clutch pressure, clutch cannon position, driveshaft speed and wheel speed can all be logged, enabling the crew chief to make a more informed choice on clutch setting for a particular pass.

Shafts and couplings

The power, once transferred through the clutch pack, must be applied to the rear axle. This is done via a steel driveshaft running from the clutch through the cannon before connecting to the reverser and finally to an output shaft coming from the rear of the reverser.

The final connection in the driveline is a very heavy-duty steel coupler that connects the reverser output shaft to the rear axle pinion.

The shafts are 300M steel – a low alloy vacuum-melted steel of very high strength. The couplings are a simple male/female slide-fit, allowing for the engine and rear end to be separated easily.

Rear-end assembly

With a lack of any suspension in a Top Fuel car, the rear axle is an integral part of the chassis. Consequently it adds to the overall chassis stiffness. The rear axle of choice in a modern Top Fuel dragster is the 12in Chrisman, the 12in referring to the crown wheel size.

The live axle design adds to the excellent structural base, maximising gear life and significantly reducing rear-end distortion. The unit is almost indestructible and features magnesium hub carriers with a spool made from steel. The crown wheel is then mounted to the steel spool. The main titanium driveshaft then passes through the centre of the spool and outwards to each of the rear hubs. These are connected to each end of the rear axle. They're made of magnesium or aluminium and are of full floating design. Each hub has five ½in studs on to which the rear wheels are mounted.

A Top Fuel dragster can make 20 passes or travel five miles before the rear axle needs servicing.

The oil used in the rear axle can vary from 140W to 220W grade and will be changed after every five runs.

The rear-end gear ratio is restricted to 3.20:1 and may be no lower or higher.

Chapter Three

European Top Fuel racing

In this section, we'll look at Top Fuel drag racing in Europe, with a full 'blow-by-blow' account of a run up the ¼ mile from four-times European Top Fuel Champion, Andy Carter. We also have an account from a crew chief's perspective, courtesy of Ben Allum.

OPPOSITE During a burnout it's vital that the dragster is kept straight and the engine rpm doesn't go up too much or drop too low. *(Dom Romney)*

In FIA European competition, the Top Fuel dragster championship is currently contested over six rounds:

- FIA Main Event, Santa Pod Raceway, England.
- Sweden Internationals, Tierp Arena, Sweden.
- FHRA Nitro Nationals, Alastaro, Finland.
- NitrOlympX, Hockenheim, Germany.
- Sweden Internationals II, Tierp Arena, Sweden.
- FIA European Finals, Santa Pod Raceway, England.

Attending the full race schedule will be dependent on the individual budget of each team. Some teams will only contest the rounds in their own country, so at some races you may see well in excess of the allowed eight-car field, all battling for a place on the ladder come race day. This obviously makes qualifying a great deal more exciting than an event with only eight cars or less entered. No one wants to be on the outside looking in on race day!

Practice

Unlike F1, there's no practice, so the first qualifying session is the first opportunity that most teams will have to see how their set-up and the track are performing. Some tracks will, however, provide a testing opportunity the weekend prior to an FIA round, with a fully prepared track and safety crew. Santa Pod will also usually provide a pro testing opportunity during the week leading up to the race. With most pro teams arriving the weekend before or during the week, this does give a perfect opportunity for shakedown passes away from full competition.

Over the Easter weekend, Santa Pod Raceway also hosts the Easter Thunderball. Although not an FIA round, Top Fuel teams are given the opportunity to blow away the winter cobwebs in an all-nitro race mixed with the Funny Cars.

Scrutineering

Upon arrival at the track, each pro team will be allocated its own pit space, with each vehicle category pitted together. With the rig in place, the teams will erect their awnings and prepare the pit space, ready to unload the trailers. As well as a working pit area for the car some teams will also have their own hospitality units, positioned adjacent to the main pit. Once everything is set up and in position, each car will need to be scrutineered before it's allowed to take part in the event. For this, an MSA (Motorsport Association) appointed scrutineer will inspect the car to ensure that all regulations are complied with and that all SFI tags are up to date. There's usually one point that the scrutineer will be very hot on with each team. Each team will also be required to produce the SFI tags for the clutch. With the introduction of the emergency shutdown system, this will also be checked for functionality.

Once passed, a sticker is placed on the vehicle to show that it's been passed to race.

The scrutineer is also required to inspect the safety wear of the driver, including their helmet, gloves, fireproof underwear, arm restraints, HANS device, boots and firesuit. Entry forms are also checked, along with the driver's individual licence.

Each driver will be required to sign on for the event and confirm their entry, following the postal entry made prior to the race. Once they've signed all the forms required for the event and scrutineering has been passed you're ready to race.

Events such as the Santa Pod Main Event actually start on Friday with qualifying for the sportsman race classes. If space allows, some pro teams may also test on this first day, subject to the approval of the race director. Most of the Top Fuel teams will use the days prior to qualifying to check through everything and perform any last-minute maintenance tasks away from the swift turnarounds required over the coming three days.

These three days will be made up of four qualifying sessions – as long as the weather doesn't affect the schedule these will usually consist of two qualifying sessions per day on the first two days; the third and final day is race day.

Qualifying

On each qualifying day the teams will face two sessions: one in the morning with a pro session start time of usually around 10:30am; and one scheduled for the afternoon, from 2:30pm onwards (times based on a typical Santa Pod Raceway schedule). During these pro sessions, the following classes will all try to qualify: FIA Top Methanol dragster, FIA Top Methanol Funny Car, FIA Pro Modified, FIA Pro Stock car, and FIA Top Fuel car. Typically the UEM bike classes will follow for their sessions.

As mentioned, the weather and other factors such as oil downs can play havoc with the schedule. This can sometimes mean very long waits in the staging lanes as the track crew frantically try to get the track into a 'go' condition. An oil down is as it sounds – a car or bike has suffered enough damage to cause an oil leak on the track. Any fluid on the race surface can be disastrous in drag racing.

Most racers will be aware of an oil-down situation and will pull their vehicle to the side of the track, therefore limiting the spread of the oil. Others, however, may not be so alert and will continue up the track, leaving a nice, neat trail behind them and causing no end of trouble for the track crew, whose clean-up job will now involve a good length of the track as well as the shutdown area at the top end. The oil is absorbed using a product not dissimilar in appearance to cat litter before the track is prepared again with the various glues and compounds used to provide the ultimate race surface. This becomes relevant to a team who may have lane choice.

Each team will be watching very carefully to see how the teams in front of them are performing so that they can see which lane might be performing better than the other. Having witnessed a clean-up in a lane it's very likely that the team with lane choice will opt for the opposite lane.

The first session of qualifying is the opportunity to come out and stamp your authority on a race with a strong qualifier 'out-of-the-box'. To achieve this, a good crew chief will be able to set the car up perfectly, with only limited data to work with at this point. Of the four qualifying passes made, your best time of the four (not your speed) will count as your qualifying time. It is these that dictate the qualifying ladder for race day. Your position within the ladder will then determine who you face in the first race.

Additional championship points are also available for the lowest ET and top speed of the event. With this in mind, qualifying is often the place to see the big numbers as teams go for the best possible position on the board, without the fear of being knocked out by the guy in the other lane if they overpower the track. In qualifying a red light on the Christmas Tree if you leave the line early doesn't matter, though if you did it on race day you'd be disqualified.

Timed runs

To get a real insight into a run in a Top Fuel dragster, I asked Andy Carter to put together a comprehensive list of what he will go through prior to, during and after a pass. I'm sure you'll agree that this is an incredible insight into the whole experience.

BELOW Race day qualifying ladder.

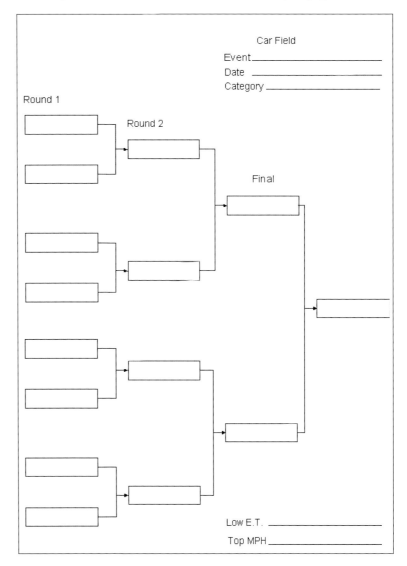

The run: a driver's perspective – Andy Carter

This is a list of the things I have to do on a typical Top Fuel run. I wrote this for myself, just to see how many things I actually have to go through, but I hope it makes interesting reading for you too. I can't give away everything, but this is 98% of what a typical run entails from my perspective.

1 The dragster has been warmed up, final checks and adjustments made and then the car is dropped down off of the air jacks. The crew wash their hands and change from their work tops into their very smart start-line tops.

2 While this is going on I'm putting on my safety gear. I put on CarbonX underwear, CarbonX socks, a firesuit and then race boots. My assistant, either Gary or Phil Cottingham, will put the rest of the kit – which consists of crash helmet, HANS device, gloves and head sock – in the tow car.

3 After checking the tow car is loaded correctly with the start-line equipment and tools needed, the crew – depending on what track we're at – will either push or tow the dragster out from under the awning of our pit area and into the staging lanes.

4 I'll get into the tow car with Phil, start to get more focused and, using the car's heater or air conditioning, will either keep warm or cool down depending on weather conditions.

5 About 30 minutes before a run I like to walk round the dragster and have a look at the wings, throttle stop, hoses, cockpit area, tyres and parachutes.

6 I walk back to the tow vehicle and start to get the rest of my kit on. This is always laid out on the back seat of the tow car.

7 Assisted by my wife Sarah, I put in the earpieces; then on with my head sock and crash helmet. Sarah makes sure the head sock is tucked into the top of my firesuit correctly, then she zips up my firesuit fully. Next it's the thick gloves on, and then finally the HANS device.

8 I walk to the left side of the car, and usually have a chat and joke with some of the team.

9 Approximately 25 minutes before the run I climb into the racecar from the left side, assisted by a crew member.

10 The crew member straps me in.

RIGHT The fully suited driver will climb into the car in the pairing lanes.
(Gary Cottingham)

FAR RIGHT The driver will be helped by a crew member, as it can often be a very tight fit.
(Gary Cottingham)

11 I check all the straps, arm and leg restraints and the HANS device for movement.

12 I check the radio with the crew chief.

13 I get comfortable and try to squash down as low as possible into the seat.

14 With my eyes closed, I try the throttle, clutch, reverser, fuel lever, parachute lever, brake, mag switches, steering and harness main buckle for position and movement.

15 I start to get really focused and relaxed.

16 I go through burnout in my head...

17 ...and then the run, at least three times.

18 I call a crew member over to pull down again on the straps now that everything's settled.

19 I focus on the run in real time.

20 At this point I can hear a crew member setting the rear tyre pressures.

21 I ask about track conditions and what's happening out there.

22 Finally it becomes my turn to run, and the officials will signal the crew to push the dragster into the start-up position just behind the water box. When doing this we make sure the dragster is lined up 100% with the groove of the track.

23 I take deep breaths, slow my heart down and relax.

24 I look up only at the track; I don't get distracted by all the stuff and the pretty women that are sometimes walking around the start-line area.

25 Focus.

26 The dragster is rocking side to side as a crew member 'backs' the motor over.

27 I can hear and feel the crew putting on the starter motor, getting the tools and gas bottle out of the tow car. The team we're racing against are doing the same in the other lane.

28 The officials have checked the track and shutdown area are safe after the last pair of dragsters have run. The Christmas Tree is set and the officials are ready, so they give the teams the signal to fire up their dragsters.

29 I have my foot off and away from the throttle, the clutch in and the brake hard on.

TOP It's now a case of waiting to be called to the collection area behind the start line.
(Gary Cottingham)

ABOVE Once called forward, the crew will manoeuvre the car into position in the collection area and wait for the signal to fire up.
(Gary Cottingham)

RIGHT The signal is given and the crew fire up the car.
(Gary Cottingham)

RIGHT Once fired up, last-minute checks are made including oil pressure and rpm. *(Gary Cottingham)*

30 Karsten Andersen reaches in and turns on the magnetos and shouts, 'Ready, Andy?'

31 I give a thumbs-up.

32 I can hear and feel the motor spinning over and then it fires on gas [petrol]. Then as they turn the fuel pump on the nitro comes through, and it's running fully on nitro. It then settles into that beautiful banging idle that only an 8,000bhp fuel Hemi motor can make!

33 As the team make fine adjustments to the fuel pump setting and let the motor go through its short warm-up, I listen to the motor carefully, making sure it's on all eight cylinders and sounding right.

34 Once the motor's running on fuel, I feel calm, relaxed and 100% ready!

35 I look at Karsten to give me the signal that he's happy with everything and I can roll forward and do the burnout.

36 I check the oil pressure and rpm.

37 I drive slowly through the water box and make small corrections to the steering to make sure I'm 100% straight with the tyre tracks and groove that I can see going up the track.

38 I let the clutch out, take the brake off, and just 20ft before the start line hit the throttle against the throttle stop and start burnout.

ABOVE Prior to the burnout the driver slowly pulls the car forward through the water box, making small corrections to the steering to ensure the car is completely straight.
(Gary Cottingham)

LEFT With the clutch out and brakes off, the driver hits the throttle against the throttle stop and starts burnout.
(Gary Cottingham)

39 I concentrate on keeping the dragster straight in the burnout and make sure the engine rpm doesn't go up too far or fall too low.

40 I come off the throttle, push the clutch in and gently brake the car to a stop.

41 I put the car in reverse...

42 ...adjust the fuel pressure if needed...

43 ...and check the oil pressure and rpm.

44 A crew member has arrived at the front of the dragster by now and starts to give the 'back up' signals.

45 I release the brake and clutch together and start to back up slowly.

46 I look to see where my competitor is.

47 Backing up straight in the centre of the

ABOVE It's vital that the dragster is kept straight during a burnout, and the engine rpm doesn't go up too much or drop too low. *(Dom Romney)*

RIGHT A crew member arrives at the front of the dragster and starts to give the 'back up' signals. *(Gary Cottingham)*

RIGHT Another crew member behind the car will help guide the driver back along the hot rubber that's just been laid down on the racing surface. *(Gary Cottingham)*

track, I make sure I keep the clutch in as much as possible to stop too much heat building up in the clutch pack.

48 Once I'm back past the start line the back-up crew member gives me the signal to stop.

49 I put in the clutch and gently pull on the brake.

50 I put the reverser back into forward gear.

51 I lift the clutch a fraction to check that I'm actually in forward gear.

52 The team are now removing the throttle stop, checking the air is on, loading the cannon, giving the rear tyres a final clean and performing all the other procedures they go through, so it's very important that my foot's off and away from the throttle, the brake is hard on and the clutch is fully in while they're in very dangerous positions around the running dragster.

53 I look down the track at the finish line.

54 The start marshal looks in at my belts.

55 I make a final check of oil pressure and rpm.

56 Karsten puts his hands in the cockpit and turns on the data logger, then squeezes my hand.

57 I check to see where my competitor is.

58 The start marshal waves us forward to pre-stage.

59 I follow my crew members' signals towards pre-stage.

60 I feather the clutch out but keep the brake dragging slightly and move slowly to the pre-stage light.

61 I'm right near pre-stage, so the crew member walks away after giving me a final good luck nod.

62 I put my helmet visor down...

63 ...and focus, focus, focus on the lights.

64 I feather the clutch, drag the brake and carefully and slowly move into pre-stage.

65 Once 'in', I hold the brake hard with the clutch fully in.

RIGHT **The driver is called forward into pre-stage.** *(Gary Cottingham)*

LEFT Once into full-stage, the driver waits for the flash of amber then releases the brake and puts throttles hard down. *(Gary Cottingham)*

CENTRE At speed, the rear tyre distortion is visible, as well as the huge force being applied to the rear wing. *(Andy Carter Collection)*

66 I check that my competitor is in pre-stage or just getting in.

67 Once we're both in pre-stage I let up the clutch and at the same time turn the fuel lever on to the 'high side', which is the fuel pump fully on.

68 I let the motor settle on the high side.

69 I check my front wheels are straight ahead.

70 Still looking at the lights, I look down the track at the finish line.

71 I release the brake slightly, and with the clutch put the dragster in 'full stage', either shallow, mid or deep depending on the situation.

72 I hold the brake really hard while making sure my competitor is now also in 'full stage'.

73 I focus on the amber light.

74 I anticipate the flash of the amber light...

75 ...and then see the flash.

76 I release the brake and hammer down on the throttle pedal.

77 I keep my right hand on the brake lever...

78 ...and make small corrections with the steering wheel to keep the car straight and in the groove.

79 I feel and listen for tyre shake, loss of traction or dropped cylinders.

80 At around 330ft and depending on how the dragster feels, I move my right hand from brake to steering wheel.

81 I continue to make small corrections with the steering while concentrating on keeping the car straight and in the groove.

82 I concentrate on the finish line.

83 I take my foot off the throttle exactly at the finish line.

84 With my left hand I push the fuel lever forward to turn off the fuel.

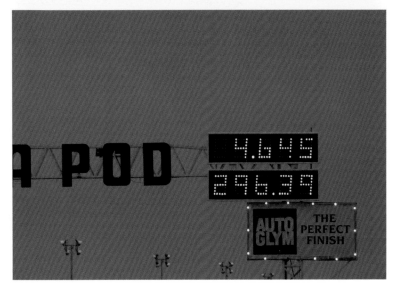

LEFT The times and speeds appear on the finish gantry and the crowd go wild. All that effort for those 4.64 seconds! *(Andy Carter Collection)*

RIGHT At the top end the fuel is turned off and both parachutes are released.

(Andy Carter Collection)

85 With both hands back on the wheel I concentrate on keeping the dragster in my side of the shutdown area.

86 I let the dragster slow some speed off, although it's still doing around 240mph at this stage.

87 With my right hand I push the parachute levers forward.

88 I feel the parachutes hit.

89 I let the car slow without using the brakes if possible.

90 Now that the fuel is off the motor will shut itself off.

91 Once the motor has stopped I turn off the magneto switches.

92 I look at the turn-off marshal for signals about turn-off.

93 I check across on my competitor, trying to see and hear where he is.

94 I make turn-off safely.

95 I gently pull the dragster to a complete stop.

96 At this point the turn-off marshals and fire crew will come over to check for fire, and shout, 'Everything alright, Andy?'

97 I answer, 'Yes, thanks!'

98 I undo my seat belts, which are always much looser at the end of the run – I think it's the large positive and negative Gs experienced during the run that make this happen.

99 I take off my gloves.

100 I take off the steering wheel...

101 ...and climb out.

102 I take off the HANS device...

103 ...my crash helmet...

104 ...and the top half of my firesuit.

105 I turn off the air bottle...

106 ...push bleed on the supercharger to release pressure...

107 ...and check the engine for oil and damage.

108 I ask turn-off marshals to wrap the parachutes around the wing for me, please.

109 I look towards the crew coming down for the tow back and we're either all very happy and cuddling if I won, or unhappy if I lost and we're out.

ABOVE With the car stopped, Andy is left to push the car off the track. I remember this specific moment – Andy is asking what he'd just run, and I had the joy of telling him 4.57 seconds at 320mph, the fastest run outside of the USA!
(Gary Cottingham)

LEFT Let's just say Karsten and crew were very happy.
(Gary Cottingham)

ABOVE This is what the fans don't get to see – the top end celebrations when it all goes well!
(Gary Cottingham)

ABOVE After each run the car will be weighed and checked and a fuel sample taken.
(Gary Cottingham)

110 Phil brings me a bottle of water.

111 He then picks up the kit I've taken off and puts it in the tow car.

112 During the tow back I talk about the run and try and find out how my competitors have done or are doing in the other pairings.

113 We tow the car to scrutineering to be weighed and have a fuel sample checked.

114 We tow the car back to our pit area and the crew start to service the whole dragster, making it ready to do it all again!

I hope you learned something out of those 114 procedures!

RIGHT The car will then be towed back to the team's pit area, where the rest of the crew will be waiting.
(Gary Cottingham)

RIGHT And the celebrations can begin. This was the scene in the pit after Carter won the 2008 title. *(Gary Cottingham)*

The run: a crew chief's perspective – Ben Allum

A s the car approaches the front of the pairing lanes I'm looking at a multitude of things.

A crew member will have been sent to measure the track temperature for me. I'll instruct a crew member as to the tyre pressure I want to run based on this information; it also feeds into the overall wealth of factors that I consider to decide the final tune-up.

I'm looking at my pager to monitor the weather conditions to see if any tune-up changes are required.

I'm taking note of the performance of the cars that are running on the track.

In recent times I've used a crew member with a lot of experience of drag racing as a whole to watch the performance of other classes, as they give a good indication of where the traction level is.

It's good to note if there have been oil downs, and if so which lane, where on the track, when they occurred and what's been down-track after the clean-up. It's true to say that these days the track crews are so good they often make the lane better with their clean-up operation, but if it's been a big one over a lot of one lane I'd choose to run in the other if I have lane choice.

Based on all this information I'll make my decisions about the tune-up. This goes on up to the last moment, the *very* last moment – it's not unusual to make adjustments between the burnout and the run.

When we're called forward the car is pushed from the pairing lanes to its starting position, looking straight down-track behind the burnout box.

A crew member is anxiously trying to get the tyres to the pressure I've requested. The game here is not to drop the pressure too early, and then for there to be a delay and a bit of cloud comes over: the tyres cool and the pressure drops too low, but the pressure still has to be spot on at the moment the car is started. I communicate with this crew member about when to get the pressures within ½lb, then within ¼lb of target, and finally I give him the signal to drop to run pressure.

ABOVE Towing down before a run. *(Gary Cottingham)*

LEFT Even at this stage work will still be going on on the car. Here Karsten cranks the motor over by hand. *(Gary Cottingham)*

The engine gets 'backed down'. This means it's cranked backwards by hand – this ensures there's no unburned fuel sitting in any of the combustion chambers which could otherwise explode when the starter motor is triggered. Fuel sitting in a cylinder in this condition has been known to blow part of the cylinder head clean off the car. This is a very dangerous situation when you have crew standing so close to the motor.

As the starter motor is fitted to the cage and connected to the battery pack I turn on CO2 and load the clutch cannon. I give the driver the signal to let him know we're going to spin the motor over to build up oil pressure. He pulls on the brake and pushes the clutch pedal down. I signal to the crew member operating the starter

BELOW A crew chief or crew member will always inspect the track surface prior to a run. (Gary Cottingham)

motor to crank the motor – he does so until I tell him to stop. I watch the dash to see the oil pressure come up. I signal the driver to let him know we have oil pressure and he can 'relax'.

All of the rotation of the motor is done with kill leads in place, which stops the ignition firing.

I make a quick check to see what is happening on track, always being mindful of what's going on with the other crew. Then we wait for the start signal. Once the signal is given to start, we turn on the data logger, turn on the ignition, arm the ignition, remove the kill leads, check the cannon is fully loaded and then…

The next step is to check with the other crew chief that they're ready – much to the annoyance of the race organisers on occasion, there's an etiquette which is (almost) always observed by (nearly) all teams to give each other as much time as possible in the case of a problem to be able to start and compete. Once the thumbs-up has been given and received I give the start signal to the driver, put a good glug of petrol into the top of the supercharger and then give the crewman on the starter motor the nod to start cranking.

Once the motor fires I feed more petrol into the supercharger from my handheld bottle, but not too much or it'll coke up the plugs and may stop; and not too little or it'll lean out and stop.

With the motor running steadily from the handheld fuel supply I open the fuel shut-offs smoothly to the fully open position and wait for what seems forever to hear the nitro feed into the motor and for that familiar, wonderful sound of a fuel motor on nitro to come through.

Fully open shut-offs are way too rich, so now the motor is running on fuel I pass my handheld fuel bottle to a crew member and set about adjusting the fuel flow to the required gallons per minute, which is displayed on the dash.

Once the fuel is set I signal the driver to move away for the burnout.

Some drivers like a signal for when to start the burnout, others like to feel the car through the box and then burnout when they decide. I prefer the former, as the driver can never see how much water the tyres have picked up. If they're soaked you want the car to roll forward further until they're just damp, but if the burnout box is a bit dry you may need to start the burnout straight away.

During the burnout I'm looking for anything untoward with the car. I watch to see how it goes up on the tyres (does it snap up hard or steadily climb up?), thinking ahead to any adjustments for the next run.

After the burnout I listen to see if the rpm settles as it should as the car rolls to a stop, and then watch to see that the driver can engage reverse (this is an especially nervous time for the clutch mechanic). It's always nice to see the car rolling back towards you at the right speed.

Crew members guide the car back to the right point on the track behind the start line. As it comes back towards me I'm looking for any problems.

Any oil leaks? – No.

Any fuel leaks? – No.

Is the rpm rate settled and steady? – Yes.

As the car's rolling backwards I walk alongside to see the dash and check the fuel volume going into the motor, and adjust it if I need to.

I check to see the CO2 system is still pressurised.

Once the car stops the crew wait to see that the driver has managed to engage forward gear, and the driver is instructed to move the car forward about 9in to clearly show it's in gear. Then he stops the car and holds steady.

Two crew members continue cleaning the slicks, which they started to do as the car was rolling backwards.

I remove the throttle stop; look to see that the appointed crew member has removed the chute safety pins; load the clutch cannon one last time and then give the signal to the crew member standing at the front of the car to beckon the driver into stage.

I move to the back of the car as it rolls forward.

Blue light on. Pre-stage.

I listen for the engine rpm to change as the fuel goes on full.

Watching the tree … watching the headers … watching the tree … looking for any fluid leaks … watching the tree … watching the headers … watching the tree … and the stage bulb is on…

The tree fires and the driver slams the throttle.

I'm watching the tree for a green light … watching the front wheels to see if they lift and watching the headers to see if any cylinders drop.

Is there any tyre shake?

Are all the cylinders lit?

Have we got traction?

ARE WE IN FRONT?

Is there any tyre shake?

Are all the cylinders lit?

Have we got traction?

ARE WE IN FRONT?

These thoughts repeat until the run is complete.

Header flames drop, the times flash up. Were we in front?

I'm immediately looking at the track for

BELOW Last-minute adjustments to the car's tuning set-up can be made in the pairing lanes.
(Gary Cottingham)

evidence of tyre shake, while listening to the car shut down to make sure everything sounds as it should.

Then my thoughts turn to 'Was there anything on that run that might have caused any damage?'

I jump in the tow car and head off to collect the car.

At the first opportunity I look to see if there are any signs of damage – the driver's body language as the crew approach in the tow car can say a lot about the run and/or any damage.

As soon as the tow car stops I jump out and retrieve the data file from the car. The crew bundle up the parachutes around the rear wing, fit the kill leads, back down the motor and if needed disengage the rear coupler. The tow rope is attached and then we're off to weigh the car, give a fuel sample, and I start to debrief the driver about the run, already thinking about what needs to be done before the next one.

Driving a Top Fuel dragster from a race fan's perspective –

Darryl Bradford

Time, age, and alcohol dim the experience of driving a Top Fuel dragster, but when I'm 65 and retired one day I'll look back on it with a wry smile.

I always have been and always will be a drag racing fan. In fact, I believe that even though I'm now a licensed Top Fuel pilot, I'm still a drag racing fan who's incredibly fortunate to have been able to experience what few others have.

Being strapped into a dragster of any kind is a strange experience. For one thing you can't move, you can't see and, to be honest, if you could you really wouldn't want to be able to turn round and look behind you!

All you can see is what's straight ahead.

You're aware of everyone looking at you but you can't see them.

Engine fired and burnout done, its time to back up carefully and slowly. A bit too slowly, I found out afterwards, because the motor was starting to get a little too much heat in it. I was concentrating more on backing up straight and not too quick so that I wouldn't stop and end up going through the water box again!

Back behind the line, and stop, clutch in and get it in forward again.

Now, that sounds easy too, but you know what it's like sitting on the sofa at home and you drop a quid down the side of the cushion? Well, imagine trying to fish it out again while being strapped in tightly: you can't look to see what you're doing and you're wearing idiot mittens just like those you wore when you were at school. There you have the basics of reaching and selecting reverse in a fueller!

Now everything happens quickly. This is like the rollercoaster going up the first steep hill to the first, and always biggest, drop! You know what's coming and you want to get off, but it's far too late for that now!

BELOW Tyre pressures will be checked right up until the last possible moment. *(Gary Cottingham)*

Forward into pre-stage: no time to think, just grab the brake as hard as you can – visor down and fuel pumps into the 'Niagara falls' position. Remember to take your foot out of the way of the clutch pedal, because if you don't the mechanical action of the clutch engaging as you go down the track brings the pedal backwards whether your foot's there or not, if you get what I mean!

What happens next is a truly religious experience of Biblical proportions.

You can never overstate what it feels like to leave the line in a Top Fuel dragster – probably because you don't know a lot about it!

The explosion of violence is horrendous, but in the most *awesome* way possible! Next time you're sat at the traffic lights in your car with the handbrake on, for a couple of seconds imagine what it would be like to have a juggernaut hit you from behind at 150mph. That would almost, *almost* give you the same feeling of acceleration; and you'd probably be in about as much control of the vehicle as well!

A modern-day Top Fuel car has a multi-stage clutch unit that comes in at pre-set points down the racetrack. This is the hardest thing to describe. Put simply, it feels like you leave the starting line about six to eight times on your way down the track. From the outside it just looks like a nice, smooth acceleration for a quarter of a mile. What it actually feels like is ten people all standing in a row, thumping you in the chest really hard at half-second intervals for five seconds! Now *this* is what it means to be alive!

As always, great things are over too quickly, which I guess is what makes them great. Before I knew it I was about 900ft down, and I took my foot away from the 'engaged' position.

The worst part about any run, as I'm sure most dragster pilots will tell you, is not the going, it's the stopping. All I did was disengage hyper drive and bang, my head suddenly felt like it weighed 50 stone and wouldn't stay upright. The worst part is that I hadn't even got the chutes out yet!

Just as I was coasting across the finish line at a rapidly decreasing rate, I hit the chutes, just as my first small problem arose – the left front tyre had, for some inexplicable reason, decided to part company with the wheel.

I must say it was a bit rough, but not too hard to keep straight. I was concentrating on getting slowed down and the fuel shut off so that the engine would cut out. Fortunately I was able to do both, and with the engine spluttering on the last dregs of fuel I pulled off the track and stopped.

The top end is a strange place. You go from being in a stress-filled, loud and crowded environment to a totally peaceful, empty field within seconds. It's almost as if it's designed that way so you can be alone with all of the thoughts that you've just had, and realise that you're breathing, tingling and just downright *alive*!

In summary, it is THE most intense, frightening, exhilarating, expensive, explosive and nerve-wracking time of your life. But think for a second – time of your *life*.

We were all born to live, so make sure you do.

After the run

As we've just seen, once the car has come to a safe stop the crew arrive on the scene to tow it back to the pit area. Before towing, they'll put kill leads on the mags, turn the air bottle off, wrap the chutes round the rear wing and turn the engine over with a bar to get rid of any fuel that might be in the cylinders. A tow rope is then attached and a crew member will steer the car back to the pit. On the way back the car will be weighed with the driver and their full gear to make sure that the car's legal; there may also be other spot checks, such as fuel and rear wing angle. Failure to comply with these will dictate that the team's qualifying pass will be discounted, or if illegal on race day disqualification will occur.

Under the right circumstances the journey back from the top end to the pit can be an awesome experience. Imagine you've just run a record-breaking 4.5-second quarter-mile ET or won the final round of the race and claimed a championship! As you head back through the pits, other racers, crew and fans all want to congratulate you on your success. Of course, if things haven't gone so well then this journey can also be one of the worst moments of the weekend!

Chapter Four

The mechanic's view

This chapter looks at Top Fuel racing from the mechanic's or crew member's perspective. I'm very grateful to three friends within the sport who have given their own account of life within a European Top Fuel crew.

OPPOSITE Gary Page is very well known in the drag racing world. Although he's usually found on crew duties these days, Page has a huge amount of experience behind the wheel, having driven at the top level in both Top Fuel and Funny Car. _(Julian Hunt)_

103
THE MECHANIC'S VIEW

If you've been round drag racing in Europe then you'll be familiar with the name Gary Page and a series of cars campaigned under the name 'Panic'. Gary is better known as a Fuel racer than a crew member, having raced in both the Top Fuel dragster and Fuel Funny Car classes. These days, however, he'll more often be found getting his hands dirty as part of the crew on a Top Fuel dragster.

Our second contributor is Sarah Senderski 'doing it for the girls'. Sarah has now worked for a number of Top Fuel teams.

The third contributor is Gareth Robinson, who worked with me previously on the hospitality/marketing side of things with Andy Carter, before stepping up to the mechanical side for Andy's last season. He's now done two full seasons on the FIA European Tour.

Gary Page

I've been around drag racing for a long time now, as I first went when I was just 12 years old, with the scouts! I loved it and soon got my brothers involved. During this time we got to know Bill Weichelt really well, who ran the Asmodeus small-block Chevy dragster. Armed with knowledge from our time around Bill, it wasn't long before we were looking to buy our own car, and so we ended up buying the ex-Mark Stratton BSA-bodied 'Hustler', which was the first 'Panic' car. This had a small-block Chevy in it and was pretty standard really, so we didn't have too much to do on it.

I started driving when I was just 17 years old. At this point we had our T-bucket car, this time with a big-block Chevy, running a very standard set-up. As we worked up through the ranks I went on to drive our Pro Comp car with its blown Chevy motor. This was when the serious work started and I got stuck into doing the clutch on that car, as well as the heads and bottom end.

As a driver, I've more recently driven Top Fuel dragsters and Funny Cars for both Rune Fjeld and Knut Söderqvist, as well as Funny Cars for Mark Hawkins, Terry Revill and Sue Collins. Just to complete the set, I've also driven in the Fuel Altered class. (A Fuel Altered is very similar in design and appearance to a Funny Car, ie it has a short wheelbase, the driver behind the motor, and a monster nitro-burning engine.

These vehicles are often based on hot-rodding favourites such as the Model T Ford or early Fiats, such as the Topolino. They're hugely spectacular, as they tend to go anywhere other than in a straight line!)

My crew experience is one that I love very much. The crew make or break the car and it's a very demanding role, as you're responsible for someone's life – that of the driver. You have to have a crew that get on well, work together well and trust each other completely. Although every crew member has their own job, it doesn't mean that that's all you do, and a good knowledge of all tasks is therefore important. I currently work on the 'bottom end' on Finnish Top Fuel racer Jari Halinen's car. Jari drives one of the four Rune Fjeld Motorsport Top Fuel dragsters that currently compete in the FIA European championship.

The bottom end is one of the least glamorous jobs on a car but is very important, as you're really looking after the heart of the engine – the crankshaft. It's dirty, and if you don't like getting covered in oil then it's definitely not the job for you. I've previously worked on the heads and have helped on the clutch, but I suppose I now specialise in bottom end. Every job is very important, as everyone has to perform their own task 100% every time for the car to run down the track. Anything less could be disastrous.

When we arrive at the track, if the car wasn't serviced at the last event we have to strip it down and service the heads and bottom end and put a new clutch in the car. We also make sure our spare heads, rods and pistons are serviced and ready to run. We'll also check over the chassis for cracks, check all the steering nuts and bolts and put the rear and front wings on the car. There's always something to do!

On race day morning we'll be at the track early, normally around 8:00am. We won't actually run until 11:30–12:00, but although the car is ready we go over everything again to make sure the car's A-OK.

We'll fire the car up around an hour and a half before we run. When we do this, we run the car on methanol to warm the engine then switch it to nitro. During this time we'll check the idle and what they call the 'tug'. This is when we put the fuel pumps on to full flow and

then let the clutch out to see what the engine pulls down to. We can adjust this by taking air bleeds out of the injector. We'll then shut the car off and adjust the valves, put the diaper (a restraining device to contain parts and fluids in the event of engine damage) and undertrays on, and the clutch will be adjusted if needed.

Again, when we go to the start line everybody has a job to do, and mine is to back Jari up after the burnout. I'm guided by another crew member behind the car, the aim being to back Jari into the tracks that he's just laid down. He'll then stop and put the car into forward and move forward a few inches. When we see this another crew member removes the throttle stop. We use this to stop the engine over-revving in the burnout. We then motion Jari into the staging beams, and after that we can do no more – it's all down to him!

After the run we go to the other end of the track and just have a quick look over the car before we remove the driveshaft so that there's no way the clutch can lock the engine up on the tow back to the pits. If this did happen it could start the engine, which isn't what you want, for obvious reasons. When the car arrives back in the pits we put it up on ProJacks to raise it. At this point things gets pretty frantic as everyone gets stuck into their allotted tasks. The undertrays and diaper are removed, the oil is taken out, the valve covers are removed, the supercharger is taken off and the clutch is removed.

I first get the rear main bearing out of the car, as this takes most of the strain. Hopefully this is OK, with no visible black marks. If there are, then we can either try to polish them out or, if it's too bad, we'll change the engine. When that's out I check Nos 4-3-2 main bearings again, and if all are OK I give them a quick wipe over and back in they go. All the rods and pistons are removed and changed and while I'm doing this the head guys are servicing them. If they're OK they'll go back on, but if not the spare heads will go on. We try to make sure the heads are the same cc as the ones we take off. The new clutch will go in and everything goes back together. This will take up around 50 minutes.

We'll put new oil and normally new plugs in the car after every run. The valves are done, the clutch adjusted and we're ready to start the car. Every crew guy is responsible for his own job and you must do that task first before everything else that might need doing. But after I'm finished I'll help lift the blower on and help

ABOVE Here Gary can be seen helping to scrub the slicks post-burnout, just prior to a run in Hockenheim.
(Julian Hunt)

with the fuel lines. We all check over the car, as sometimes when you're rushed you'll miss doing things, but someone else will always pick it up. I know of a few instances where crews have forgotten to put oil in the car or have left a plug loose.

It's a very hard job, being on a Top Fuel crew, but each member must do their job right every time for the car to achieve a low four-second, 300mph run over 1,000ft.

We then run the car and do it all over again! As I said, it's very hard work, and everyone works for everyone else, and although you have a job to do you'll still do anything to help any of the other crew guys and make sure the car's 100% safe for your driver.

Sarah Senderski

I first entered the Top Fuel pits when I was around 12 years old. I remember my dad asking me, 'Do you fancy going to Santa Pod to watch some drag racing?' – I'd always worked on cars with my dad since being a small child, from riding around on his lap during the parade laps in his stock car to stripping and rebuilding an old Mini in our garage. I never imagined what an effect that day at Santa Pod would have! The first whiff of nitro and the

sound of the engines as they roared into the burnout left me speechless … from then on I was hooked. My dad will tell you how annoying it actually was to go and watch with me. I was forever sniffing around the pits, watching the crew guys frantically stripping down the engines and thrashing to make the next round. I was often seen in the pits watching at 3:00 in the morning, not wanting to leave even to eat, shower or go to sleep! I started speaking to Smax Smith when he was racing his Funny Car and often watched him frantically trying to fix it. It was funny, as I was never really interested in the driving aspect – to me it was all about being on the crew, and being one of the guys responsible for building one of these monsters. I desperately wanted to be one of the guys stood on the start line waiting for the car to launch, thinking 'Yeah, I'm part of this.'

My chance came when I was invited into Smax's pit to help out with his Top Fuel dragster. I couldn't believe it – I finally had the opportunity to get involved and play with a dragster! I think they were a little sceptical, I mean, who expects a young teenage girl to turn up at their pits and want to get her hands dirty? But the guys I spent the weekend with were brilliant, and once they realised I was actually kinda useful I was well away!

The guys running the car were starting up their own team the season after, and I was asked if I wanted to help out. Of course, I leapt at the chance! I started out doing jobs like cleaning out the oil pan and refuelling the car, but at the end of the day they could have had me doing any job, because as far as I was concerned I was living my dream. Then the day came when one of our cylinder head mechanics wasn't able to come to one of the races, and I was volunteered to take on his job for the race. I've never been so scared in all my life! It seemed like an impossible task, but I was so excited I don't think I slept for the whole week before the race. The first strip and rebuild was so intense I don't think I could remember what actually happened, but I knew for sure I wanted to do it again. I'd never ached so much (torquing cylinder heads down to 170ft/lb is a pretty mean feat for a 16-year-old girl). But the most surprising thing to me was how quickly I got into the swing of things, and soon I was

BELOW As well as Shelley Pearson bringing girl power to Top Fuel as a driver, Sarah Senderski is doing her bit in the pits as a crew member.
(Julian Hunt)

seeing firing orders and setting valve clearances in my sleep.

The first moment I stepped out in front of the car to back it up was also an unforgettable experience. I think my legs pretty much went to a jelly state and the words 'Whatever you do, make sure your shoes are tight, and for goodness sake don't fall over!' echoed in my head (some kind words of advice from my crew chief).

From this point on I never wanted to miss another race, and since then I've worked on many different teams and travelled to most of the European tracks. If you'd told me I would be doing this all those years ago I think I'd have laughed in your face.

I've now worked on many different teams throughout my time in Top Fuel, and despite the many differences between them the main principle is still the same: you want to fix the car and get it down the track. No matter how much pain you're in from the manic exhaustion of the rebuilds or the extreme fatigue from lack of sleep, you manage to pull through and somehow end up on the start line ready to see the car run again. The main drawback is that just a few seconds later you have to do it all over again (although you never actually know what to expect when the car comes back to the pits…).

Each crew member has their own responsibility on the car. Each person knows exactly what to do and in what order. It may sometimes look like organised chaos, with tools flying around in the air and people clambering over each other (the guy working on the bottom of the engine always manages to get a face full of nitro or a foot in his side), but I can assure you somewhere in all that there's a plan, and it will inevitably come together to get the car to the start line. After a few runs through with your crewmates you can pretty much second-guess who'll do what and in what order, and somehow it all comes together from organised mayhem to a streamlined process. Down to the last clip on the last body panel, everyone knows their specific tasks.

Each crew member will have their own part of the car to look after. There are usually two people working on the cylinder heads with another servicing and building the spare sets between rounds. Then there are usually one or two people doing the bottom end of the engine

(the guy rolling around on the floor getting nitro in his eyes and kicked in the ribs by the cylinder head people) and two clutch guys. The clutch guys are always recognisable, as they're the ones who are almost invisible in the dark, as they're covered from head to toe in clutch dust (a mysterious substance that's almost impossible to get out of your skin). There also have to be other people doing jobs ranging from mixing fuel to servicing the supercharger and fixing/fabricating the bits that have broken/melted/been destroyed – the list is endless. It seems that on a Top Fuel team there can never be enough hands on deck.

The task of stripping an engine down to the block and rebuilding it again, in time for a warm-up and to make the next round, is no mean feat.

I'm a cylinder head mechanic, so I have the manic task of stripping and rebuilding half of the engine down to the block after each run. Another guy does the other side (the V8 design lends itself quite nicely to that). I've done this role for many years, and have managed to prove myself in this largely male-dominated sport (though I do still get the odd surprised look when I torque the cylinder heads down or carry a cylinder head across the pit).

As a team, the main thing we all need to be sure of is that the car we're sending down the track is put together and all the right bits are in the right places. Even though we've stripped and rebuilt the car many, many times, there's still room for slight mistakes. When

ABOVE Sarah is a cylinder head mechanic and has the task of stripping and rebuilding half of the engine down to the block after each run.
(Julian Hunt)

you're finishing rebuilding the engine at 3:00 in the morning you can understand how fatigue might get in the way! As a team we all have to try and do our own job but also be aware of what's going on around us so that we can get it right first time. I'm always checking in with the guy on the opposite side of the engine, making sure we're doing everything correctly and to the same standard. It seems no matter how many times you double-check that you're using the right 'cold' valve clearance setting you're never actually sure!

It's extremely important that every part of the engine is checked every time it comes apart, as even the slightest defect can be terminal when you're trying to make 8,000bhp stick to the track. That slightly worn lifter roller can certainly prove to be an engine breaker.

When it comes to lining up on the start line your mind is literally racing before the engine has even been turned over. Are the spark plug leads in the right number cylinder and the right way round? (Actually a pretty common error – if you ever hear a pop and a bang as the car is cranked over and then the frantic removal of leads by confused crew members, that's usually the source of the problem.) Are all the correct nuts in place and torqued down properly? Are there any random leads caught in places where they shouldn't be? Is the blower belt tension as good as you want? Are all the body panels secure and going to stay in place? As you can see, the list is exhaustive.

However, things can and do go wrong. There's nothing worse than seeing your car launch and then go up in smoke. Don't get me wrong, it makes for an amazing show when you see an 8,000bhp machine literally blow itself to bits in seconds, but the reality is that behind that there's a crew and a driver who potentially may not race again that weekend, if not the rest of the season. I remember being stood on the start line with one of the cars and as it got to about halfway down the track the clutch pretty much exploded, resulting in an enormous fireworks display as it melted itself into a million pieces. The walk back to the pits after that run was somehow not long enough. I don't think a single one of us actually wanted to see what state the car was in when we got back.

It's been said so many times that ours is a sport of highs and lows. It's such a sorry sight to see your car limp back to the pits, and the reality is you never know what you're going to see when you start taking it apart. There's no real rule of thumb. Sometimes you expect to see a complete mess when you start taking things apart and end up with a fairly clean engine, and other times the slightest little 'blip' and the entire engine can need replacing. But somehow you manage to all pull together as a team and get that car race-ready again.

It happened to us on one of the teams a few years ago. We were racing with relatively few spare parts and we'd managed to already destroy two engine blocks just in qualifying. But we qualified well and wanted to go out on race day. We managed to find the least damaged block with the most potential for repair and set to work machining it and then rebuilding the car. However, this was such a mammoth task that we ended up finishing setting the valves at 5:00am, and with only an hour's sleep we were up again to do the final checks before the first run. We were destroyed, but as soon as we fired the car up for the warm-up we all somehow found a new lease of life and were ready to race. As luck would have it we got through the first round and set a new team personal best in the semi-final. That left the final. Surely a team who were up all night because we nearly had to quit the race couldn't win the final? Well, we did. And I don't think a single one of us could believe it as we watched the car sprint into the distance and the winning lights illuminate. But that's the crazy thing about our sport – you can never actually be sure *how* things will end up. Sure, you can have the biggest teams with the most money winning race after race, but you can still see the underdog rookie teams going out and making their mark in the field.

Gareth Robinson

From my early days of following the sport I'd always watched and followed the career of the UK's Andy Carter, and it was through Andy that I first got involved with a Top Fuel team.

It was back in 2009, just before the FIA European Finals, that a 'Crew member required' advert was placed on the Eurodragster.com website. The role was to join the Carter Motorsport hospitality team. As soon as I finished reading the article I was eagerly writing an email to apply for the role, and a few days later I had a reply saying that they were keen to have me join their team.

With the 2010 season upon us, I found myself eagerly watching the Andersen Racing Top Fuel team hard at work turning their car round. I was amazed, and all the time kept thinking, 'I want to be in there doing that, but I have no chance.' However, as the season came to an end it was announced that Andy was going alone and starting a new team of his own for 2011. Was this my chance to shine? You bet it was!

In the early part of 2011 I spent almost every weekend hard at work in the workshop helping Andy and the rest of the guys set up the new team. It was at this time that I was approached by Andy's crew chief, Ben Allum. Would I like to step up my role and work on the car? It didn't take long for the answer to roll off my tongue and the biggest grin ever to appear on my face.

I spent all of 2011 working for Andy until his retirement at the end of the season. Having only done one season I couldn't call it a day, so for the 2012 season I joined the F&A Racing Top Fuel team.

How does a crew work?

Each crew member should have a good knowledge of how an engine works and have a reasonable level of mechanical skill, though that isn't always necessary as most teams will give you the training you need to do a particular job or role on the car.

You need to be able to work well as a team player and under pressure. In the European races you have around 90 to 120 minutes to fully service the car ready for the next round. Before you know it that time has gone and one of the track staff is at your pit calling you to the pairing lanes.

Each crew member has to have trust in all the others and know that they've performed their set roles to the highest standard. One thing you have to remember is that this is a Top Fuel engine and not your average family car engine – Top Fuel engines aren't so forgiving when something isn't done right or goes wrong!

LEFT Gareth Robinson originally cut his teeth in the crew as part of the hospitality team with Andy Carter. Even then it was clear that his desire was to work on the car, and when the opportunity came Gareth took it with both hands.
(Gary Cottingham)

BELOW As the car is pushed back into the pit, the crew are fully aware of the thrash that's ahead of them.
(Mark Skinner)

RIGHT It's hard to believe that the car is stripped to the block after every run, with everything checked and serviced before being put back together again. Here the blower is removed from the inlet manifold ready to be serviced. *(Mark Skinner)*

RIGHT Once removed and in position, the supercharger can undergo the checks required to the lobes and mechanisms. *(Mark Skinner)*

Top Fuel tasks

Most Top Fuel teams are arranged in pretty much the same way:

Supercharger technician

During the service (turnaround) the blower technician will assist the cylinder head technicians with the removal of the blower from the car. Once the blower is on the workbench the technician will be in charge of checking and fully servicing the blower ready for the next run.

Cylinder head technicians

As the engine is a V8 you need a separate person for each side of the engine.

At the start of the turnaround the cylinder head technicians will start their initial stripdown of the heads before turning their attention to the blower. They'll work together to get the blower safely off the car, with assistance from the blower technician to safely lift it clear. Once

RIGHT As well as being accessible from the underside, the end casing can also be removed for easy access. *(Mark Skinner)*

FAR RIGHT Pistons will be prepared in the trailer, ready to be used as required. *(Mark Skinner)*

ABOVE **The cylinder heads will be removed, serviced and cleaned between each run...** (Mark Skinner)

ABOVE AND LEFT **...as well as the gaskets, before being mounted back in place.** (Mark Skinner)

this is out of the way they'll then turn their attention back to the removal of the heads.

Once the heads are off the car the next things to come out are the pistons. This will usually be done with one of the cylinder head technicians and one of the 'floaters' (see page 113), while the other cylinder head technician will start the service of the heads before they can go back on the car.

Clutch technician

All the crew members are important but the clutch technician is probably one of the most important. No matter how well the rest of the engine is put together, if this job isn't done right the car simply won't go down the track.

When the car comes back from a storming run everything is extremely hot, especially the clutch. Nevertheless, the clutch technician will start to strip the clutch down immediately after the run. Once the bellhousing is off, all of the heat built up on the run escapes from the

FAR LEFT **Adjustments are made to the clutch cannon by the clutch technician.** (Mark Skinner)

LEFT **The clutch is a hugely dirty job as well as a hot one! Here part of the clutch assembly is cleaned using an airline to remove clutch dust.** (Mark Skinner)

RIGHT One of the
most unenviable
tasks on the car is
the bottom end. This
is the bottom end
technician's view as he
services the lower half
of the engine.
(Mark Skinner)

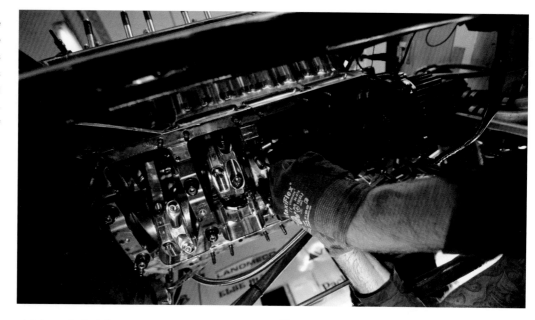

clutch, and all of the other crew members feel it! Next to come out are the clutch discs and floaters. The heat that comes off of these is so intense that you could instantly cook an egg on them. The clutch technician will have to remove these from the car and put them out of the way of the crew and spectators.

Once the clutch is fully stripped down and cleaned, the clutch technician will start the rebuild – a delicate process of setting up ready for the next run.

Bottom end technician (or 'diver')

The bottom end technician is in charge of servicing the bottom half of the engine. This involves the removal of the undertray and diaper first. Next they'll need to get the oil pan off the engine ready for inspection of the main cap bearings. This needs to be done in a fairly short space of time, as if they find damage to the crank they'll need to let the crew chief know ASAP, as this will determine whether the engine is going to have to come out or not.

RIGHT With the oil pan
completely removed
it can be inspected
for any objects that
shouldn't be there but
are present as a result
of engine damage on a
run. *(Mark Skinner)*

FAR RIGHT Once
checked the pan will
be fully cleaned before
being replaced by the
bottom end technician.
(Mark Skinner)

If everything is OK with the bearings they'll then need to make a start on the removal of the pistons. This can't be done until the cylinder head technicians have fully removed the heads.

While the cleaning of the top deck of the engine is being handled by the cylinder head technicians, the bottom end technicians will get the replacement set of pistons ready to go into the motor and make a start on servicing the ones that have just been removed from the engine.

Once all the cylinder head technicians have finished the cleaning, the bottom end technician will make a start with the rebuild and installation of the new pistons.

Floaters

Most teams will also have a couple of people known as floaters. The role of a floater is just as important as those servicing the rest of the engine. A floater might be used in a number of roles around the car during the service to assist the other crew members.

ABOVE LEFT The bottom end technician will be required to inspect the main cap bearings as well as the crank. If the crank's damaged then the crew chief will need to know ASAP, as this will dictate the engine coming out completely.
(Mark Skinner)

ABOVE He'll also be required to remove the pistons once the cylinder head technicians have removed the heads.
(Mark Skinner)

LEFT It's fair to say that the bottom end isn't a glamorous place to be in a Top Fuel pit, but each crew member has their task which must be fulfilled with commitment and precision.
(Mark Skinner)

ABOVE **Once everything's been removed and inspected it's time to put it all back together again...** *(Mark Skinner)*

BELOW **...which with limited time between rounds can sometimes be a real race against the clock.** *(Mark Skinner)*

For example, once the car is up on stands and the stripdown has started they may be asked to help the bottom end technician. This could mean dropping the oil out of the pan while the bottom end person starts to undo the oil pan. The next thing might be getting the oil pan clear of the car; this is where it gets dirty. This will be checked for any fragments of metal that could provide vital information for the tuner.

What do I look after?

My own main role on the car is left cylinder head technician. However, I can from time to time drop into another role at the workshop, in between race meetings or sometimes at the track. These roles could be mixing the fuel, packing the parachutes or, on the odd occasion at the workshop, servicing the bottom end.

As a cylinder head technician I'd also be responsible for the building of racks of pistons during down time, building sets of cylinder heads and other mechanical parts used in the heads and valve train.

A typical turnaround for me would go something like this (assuming there's no major damage to the engine):

The car will come back to the pits and instantly I'll get into my zone and block out the world beyond the pit area for two hours to focus on the service.

Once the car is up in the air, I'll make a start by removing all of the ignition leads and spark plugs from the side of the engine, putting the plugs in order in the top end tray ready for inspection by the tuner.

I'll then start to remove the valve cover, trying not to let hot oil drip down on to the bottom end technician.

Next I'll start to undo the fuel lines and ancillaries from the blower, and working with the other cylinder head technician we'll start to release the blower from the engine. Once the blower is out of the way I make a start on stripping the cylinder head down ready for its removal. By this time the clutch is well on its way out of the car and you're hit by a sudden heat wave and the sweat starts to pour from you.

Once I've fully released the cylinder head from the car it's time to remove it. This is where it's important that the crew has gelled together well,

and everybody knows where each crew member is at any one time during the turnaround.

The heads are heavy, bulky things that are hot and dripping with hot oil. I shout 'Head coming off the car,' so that the rest of the crew hear me and allow me a clear path through. With one swift, straight pull I have the head off the engine and make my way round the car to the cylinder head workbench, so that it's ready for servicing.

Back to the car – I then install my sleeve locks and make a start with the removal of the pistons from the engine.

I return to the heads and start to fully clean them ready for servicing. By this time the new pistons have been installed into the engine. I'll then make a start on cleaning the top deck ready for refitting of the heads.

Once the heads are placed on the motor, both cylinder head technicians will make a start at bolting them back on. Once this is done we'll refit the blower. By now the bottom end will be back together and the clutch built to the point where we can start to turn the motor over by hand. We turn the motor over a couple of times just to check that everything is OK. We then make a start on setting up the valve train, also known as the 'valve lash'.

By this time everybody will be at the point where we're ready to start the motor, known as the warm-up. Once we're ready to go the starter goes on to the car. Even though you've built this engine time and time again with no issues, it always plays on your mind – have you done it right this time? The motor is spun over for oil pressure, and once we're happy we nod to fire it up. By now we've all got our ear defenders and gas masks on (yes, that's right, gas masks: once nitromethane is burnt it turns into tear gas).

A drop of fuel down the injector and a split second later the engine fires up. At the start it will just tick over from a barrel of methanol while a few checks are made. Once happy, the crew chief will pull the fuel pump on and the beast really jumps into life as she starts to gulp gallons

of nitro. By this time you start to lose your vision, as the pit begins to turn into a strong yellow haze as the tent fills with nitro fumes. Once all the checks are complete the engine is shut down.

ABOVE After a few minutes to get cleaned up the crew will put on their 'start-line shirts' ready to tow the car down to the start line. Prior to this the crew chief will give the crew a full briefing.
(Gary Cottingham)

I then remove the spark plugs and leads from the engine ready to remove the valve cover. Once this is off, I work closely with the other cylinder head technician to do another 'valve lash' check, known as the 'hot lash'.

Finally I put the valve covers back on and finish the last couple of jobs ready to take the car into the pairing lanes.

The service is complete and the car's on its way to the track. Once we get the call from the track staff to pull round to the start line, I help with starting the car. Once again a special mix of fuel is poured down the injector hat and the engine's cranked over. The motor fires into life, and this time without the barrel of methanol it goes straight on to nitro. The engine has now started that famous fuel motor cackle. The chief starter signals for the driver to draw forward into the water box and starts the famous but very important smoky burnout. With the start line filled with tyre smoke and flying bits of rubber from the tyres, the driver starts to reverse.

By now the tyre smoke has hopefully started to disappear, and the 8,000bhp beast is coming towards me at over 50mph. It comes to a stop and a slight forward movement. I take the biggest lungful of fresh air I can get and move in to sweep the right-side tyre and look for any leaks (which we don't want, as that'd be our race over). I now have the pressure from the engine thumping into the side of my head and my lungful of fresh air is starting to run out. My eyes are streaming with tears from all the nitric acid fumes and I move back, away from the car, and get over to the left side. I try to take another lungful of air but it's

mostly nitro fumes, and I crouch down as the car goes into pre-stage. The driver then pulls the engine over on to the high side and the fuel pump is now fully open and the sound of the motor starts to die down. The driver gently pulls the car into stage and the Christmas Tree starts its countdown. Then there's a hell of a boom as the two competing 8,000bhp+ Top Fuel dragsters launch into the distance.

At this point I'm trying to keep an eye on the left cylinder that I've just put on the car. I'm looking to see if all of the cylinders stay alight and hopefully I won't see any flames coming from my side of the engine. If I see a green flame start to appear I know I've got my work cut out, as the car has started to torch the cylinder head.

It's all over and I'm on my way back to the pits to get ready to start the service process all over again. Fingers crossed the engine is still in one piece with minimal damage.

On returning to the pit area, each crew member will have their own set of things to look out for during the service of the car that, if missed, could cause complications during the rebuild or cause damage to the engine on the run.

The most important thing is safety. Although we're all focused on turning the car round ready for the next run, we're also all looking out for each other. When we're servicing the car, space is limited between crew members and injuries could easily happen. However, we all know where each crew member is, and we can all work round each other with the minimum of interference.

What can go wrong and why?

With a Top Fuel engine there are a lot of things that can go wrong, and sometimes for no apparent reason. By now we've taken the engine apart and rebuilt it time after time with no cause for concern, but the most common problem is simply the mechanical failure of parts.

One of the most annoying things that can go wrong on the run itself is the blower belt snapping. The blower is one of the vital parts of a Top Fuel engine, and without it the car's going nowhere. As a belt drives the blower from the crankshaft, it's vital that it stays intact on the run. It'll have been checked during the service, or even swapped for a brand new one, so that hopefully there's no cause for concern. But if it snaps it can do a lot of damage around the front of the engine. It spins around at very high rpm, and in between the belt are the fuel pump and fuel lines, which could easily be damaged. One of the most common things that the belt will damage is the starter cage around the front of the blower.

If you have a mechanical parts failure within the cylinder head this can be the start of an expensive run. For example, if you damage a valve during the run the chances are that things are going to go bang in a big way. If a piston ring starts to break up on the run, then the movement of the piston will throw around parts of the ring, and if just one small piece of it was to get stuck between an intake valve and its seat it'll cause the valve to stick open. Now, with the valve stuck open it leaves an open route into the blower manifold where the fuel's distributed to all of the cylinders. When it's time for a cylinder to fire with the valve stuck open it ignites the fuel in the cylinder, as well as all the fuel in the manifold, and then *BANG* – it blows the blower off the car in a large fireball. This is spectacular for the trackside photographers and spectators, but a nightmare for the crew, who now could have a long night's work ahead of them.

Another thing that can go wrong is that the engine could kick a rod out the side of the block. This can happen if the piston breaks free from the connecting rod, leaving the rod to move around with the momentum of the crankshaft. The trouble is the rod now has no fixed route that it can take until it jams into the side of the block and smashes a hole through the side. This is then followed by a large trail of fire as the oil ignites. In turn, this causes a lot of damage, burning wires, sensors and other hardware around the rear of the car.

You can also have issues with the clutch. One of the common things that can go wrong is that the clutch locks up too early at the start of the run and causes the car to smoke the tyres. This is one thing you don't want come race day, as the chances are your race is over right at the start.

What are the highs?

For me there are a lot of highs in Top Fuel drag racing. These are just a couple of personal highs that mean a lot to me:

The main one for me is the fact that I'm here working on a Top Fuel car. I class myself as one of the lucky few who get to do this. I got to work for Andy Carter after having spent years watching his Top Fuel career. Albeit for only one race, I also got to work with one of the most famous racers/tuners in European drag racing, Peter Lantz. I've also got to meet a lot of great people and made a lot of good friends within the European drag racing scene.

The next obvious high is winning rounds, hopefully followed by winning the meeting. Of course, the ultimate high is to win the championship.

Another of the highs for me – and one that's hard to explain in words – is standing there on the start line between two Top Fuel dragsters as they launch from the line.

The list could go on and on!

And the lows?

Again, there can be a lot of lows within this great sport. One of the real lows for any team is a slight misjudgement by the driver pulling a red light on the Tree. All that hard work gone to waste and you lose a race before it's even started!

The most *annoying* low for any team is the weather. There's nothing worse than travelling halfway across Europe to sit around the pits all weekend and not even get on the track due to bad weather. Unlike F1 or Touring cars, etc, we can't just put wet weather tyres on the cars and go racing.

BELOW The reason why the crew do it – the celebration of a race win or, even better, a championship win! *(Gary Cottingham)*

Chapter Five

The crew chief's view

The crew chief is the most important part of any Top Fuel crew, as it's their decisions that will ultimately determine the success or failure of any run in the car. They decide what tuning set-up will be used on the car, as well as guiding the rest of the crew through their duties and, most importantly, working closely with the driver to obtain as much feedback as possible on any pass. It's a massive obligation, as not only is the performance their responsibility but so is the safety of the driver, crew and public at the racetrack.

OPPOSITE Ben and the Phoenix crew prior to a pass at the NHRA race. This was to be a tough experience for Allum and the team. *(Ben Allum Collection)*

119

RIGHT All Top Fuel teams operate from their own rig at the racetrack.
(Mark Skinner)

BELOW The trailer will be fully loaded with everything required for the race weekend.
(Mark Skinner)

A successful crew, as with any team discipline, functions best with clear leadership, with each individual being fully aware of their duties and what's expected of them. There's no place for a crew member who wants to do it his way, as ultimately they have to respect and accept the crew chief's authority without question.

For the continued harmony of the team it also helps if everyone gets on well, as, particularly in Europe, budgets are tight, so many race rigs are equipped with bunk areas for the crew. These guys really *are* in each other's pockets at any race meeting.

A typical Top Fuel crew will consist of:

- Tuner
- Crew chief
- Driver
- Two top end technicians
- One bottom end technician
- Two clutch technicians
- One supercharger technician
- Two floaters

As well as their specific duties, at least one crew member will also drive the truck, with others driving the support vehicles for each event.

All Top Fuel teams operate from their own rig at the racetrack. The team trailer will be loaded with everything required for the race weekend and fully equipped with workbenches, generators, airlines and tools to perform as many tasks as possible in the pits. There are no garages at the tracks in Europe, apart from Hockenheim, Germany, where the TF teams are privileged to be able to use the F1 garages as their base for that particular meeting.

As well as the rig trailer unit, each

ABOVE As well as the rig trailer each team will also have a full-length awning that extends out from the trailer, doubling the overall footprint of their workspace. *(Mark Skinner)*

ABOVE Each area of the trailer is used to help create the best possible working environment, including bench space, sinks and tunes. *(Mark Skinner)*

LEFT The teams will use a ProJack racecar stand, an air-operated lifting jack worked by a foot pedal. Jacks are placed at the front and rear of the car before elevation. *(Mark Skinner)*

team will also have a full-length awning that extends out from the trailer, therefore doubling the overall footprint of the available workspace.

The dragster will be removed from the trailer on arrival and pushed into position under the awning. Most teams will put down some form of pit flooring before this is done. Once in place, the teams will use a ProJack racecar stand, which is an air-operated lifting jack operated by a foot pedal. Jacks are placed at the front and rear of the car before elevation. The Top Fuel dragster will spend most of its weekend suspended in this way, making it easy for the crew to get around and under the car.

With the car in position, a number of tables or workbenches will be set up along the outside edge of the awning and alongside the trailer, providing workspace for maintenance

BELOW The Top Fuel dragster will spend most of its weekend suspended in this way, making it easy for the crew to get around and under the car. *(Mark Skinner)*

LEFT With the car in position, a number of tables and workbenches will be set up along the outside edge of the awning and alongside the trailer. *(Mark Skinner)*

CENTRE Each team will have at least one support vehicle, and sometimes two. *(Mark Skinner)*

BOTTOM A support vehicle is used to head to the top end after a run to collect the driver and the car. The Andersen Racing team have a golf buggy that's used for this purpose. *(Mark Skinner)*

on items such as the cylinder heads, supercharger etc.

As well as the rig a team will have at least one support vehicle, sometimes two. This vehicle gives the driver space in which to prepare himself ahead of a race, both mentally and in terms of donning his required safety wear. It's also used to collect him from the top end after a run, and, since a Top Fuel dragster can't just start up and trundle down to the start line, the support vehicle is used to tow it there. Any vehicle towing needs to have a large enough space to carry the starter motor and a small selection of tools. This vehicle will tow the car down the fire-up road prior to the run and collect it from the top end, as well as tow it back to the pits. In addition support vehicles are often used as an opportunity to promote the team's sponsors and are usually painted in the team's full livery.

The spares carried by a team vary depending on their overall budget. Top Fuel drag racing is expensive so it's fair to say that big-budget teams will obviously be the best prepared and carry the most spares. By contrast, the small-budget teams may very well have to 'beg, borrow, and steal' all that they can in order to go racing. Such teams would carry a minimum of spares, usually including spare rods, pistons, valves, plugs, lubricants and fuel at the least. Darryl Bradford writes elsewhere in the book about his Top Fuel experience, and he and his team openly admit that they were one of the low-budget teams. Darryl recalls that they did have a spare engine block, but it didn't have any liners or studs. It's common for a Top Fuel car to put a rod through a block, so a spare would mean that parts could be removed from the damaged one and added to the replacement.

In European racing there are some team owners who carry spares that can be purchased by other teams if required. These may not be the best on the market, and more often than not they'll be used, but they're good enough to get you through the meeting until a better replacement can be procured. Things like cranks, which cost in excess of $7,000 a time, can often be purchased in the pits for a fraction of the cost; the replacement would be a used item and probably an ex-US team part, and you'd probably end up paying around $1,000 for it. If budgets are *very* tight then such items might even be procured at the commencement of an event but only paid for once the weekend's appearance money was paid out by the event promoter at its conclusion. It's not ideal, but at least you'd be racing!

In my experience, if a spare is needed then a trip round the various other team pits with hard cash would usually result in a replacement being found. This, I believe, shows great camaraderie between the teams on the European tour, as the desire to see all the cars out on track outweighs any advantage in seeing a rival out of the competition simply through a lack of parts.

Teams operating on a much larger budget can carry almost everything in duplicate, from ready-built spare motors to a complete spare chassis. It really is down to each individual budget. 'Hot Rod' Fuller was a leading light in the NHRA Top Fuel championship before heading to Abu Dhabi and the famous Yas Marina circuit. He now drives one of their own cars, which are run under stellar budgets. I recall an interview with him soon after he made the switch, stating that the trailer carried six complete spare motors ready to be dropped in should they be required!

One of the best things about drag racing from a fan's perspective is the open pits. There's no charge to enter, and fans can easily wander around and watch the crews as they work on their vehicles. Depending on how hectic things are at the time, the crews will happily chat to fans and explain the tasks they're performing or what's required to run a

car of this nature. However, one time when it's best not to approach a team is between rounds on race day!

I mentioned earlier that a car will spend most of its weekend up on its stands. This is because after every run made, the car must be returned to the pits and completely stripped down to the bare block before being built back up again. What makes this even more incredible is not only the level of work done but also the time in which the crews can achieve it. In Europe, a crew will be given two hours to get things done. In America the time allowed is 90 minutes, but a good time is around the 75-minute mark. Ben Allum, Carter Motorsport crew chief in 2005, recalls a best turnaround time of *45 minutes*! This was in Finland, to make the final. The team went on to win the race and you can read a full account of the experience later in this chapter.

Besides simply dismantling the engine and putting it back together, each part will be carefully inspected for damage, and parts on a limited run life will be discarded and replaced. The pressure is huge, of course, not only because the clock is ticking but also because safety aspects must be considered, and there's no room for error. The slightest mistake could be the trigger that detonates the 8,000bhp bomb that's sat just behind the driver's head! This is where the driver must put complete trust in his crew to deliver without mistakes that could be costly not just in terms of safety but also in points and championships.

The moment the car is up on the stands, the crew begin their thrash in a manner that often looks chaotic; but each member knows their task and the operation is carefully coordinated. Yes, there'll be the odd bash into each other as duties are performed in tight spaces, or the odd spill of hot oil, but that's part of the job and the team simply get on with it. I've witnessed red-hot clutch discs accidentally dropped out of a clutch assembly only centimetres away from the head of another crew member working beneath the car! These guys really do earn their money (though in fact most European crews are unpaid), and I believe they're some of the most dedicated mechanics in motorsport.

The following list should give you a good idea of the timing of the operation and the tasks faced:

■ The car is brought into the pits. The crew start to pull off the side panels.
■ The tool organiser is put in place on top of the driver's roll cage. The plug wires and fuel lines begin coming off.
■ The ballistic covers are removed from the engine. The puke tank is removed.
■ The valve covers come off.
■ The rear wheels are removed. The oil pan is drained and removed.
■ The blower is removed.
■ The first main bearing cap comes off.
■ The rocker-arm system is taken off of the heads.
■ The cylinder heads are taken off.
■ The first rod cap is taken off.
■ The first piston and rod assembly is removed from the engine. The cylinder head men begin checking cylinder bores as the pistons come out.

BELOW The tool organiser is put in place on top of the driver's roll cage. *(Mark Skinner)*

BOTTOM The rear wheels are removed. *(Mark Skinner)*

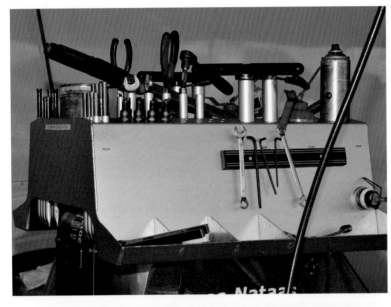

BELOW The oil pan is drained and removed. *(Mark Skinner)*

ABOVE The rocker-arm system is taken off the heads. *(Mark Skinner)*

LEFT The blower is removed. *(Mark Skinner)*

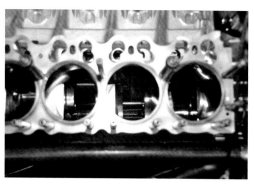

ABOVE The first piston and rod assembly is removed from the engine. *(Mark Skinner)*

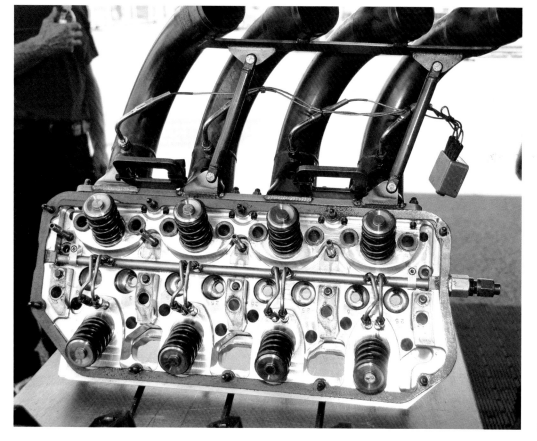

LEFT The cylinder heads are taken off. *(Mark Skinner)*

- Bellhousing removed.
- The final piston/rod assembly comes out. Replacement of the lower bearing shells in the main bearing caps commences.
- The final clutch pieces come out.
- The lifters are removed.
- A new clutch pack goes in.
- The first of the new piston/rod assemblies goes back in.
- The last piston/rod is installed. The final main bearing cap and bearing shell are checked.
- The last main bearing cap bolt is torqued.
- The bottom end is buttoned up, including the pan.
- The head gaskets are put back in place.
- The first cylinder head is put back in place.
- The pushrods are installed.
- The rocker-arm assembly is bolted down.
- Engine oil is poured through the lifter valley.
- The belt and pulley system is installed.
- The intake manifold is put back in place and checked for flatness.

TOP The bellhousing is removed. *(Mark Skinner)*

LEFT The first of the new piston/rod assemblies goes back in. *(Mark Skinner)*

BELOW LEFT The last piston/rod is installed. *(Mark Skinner)*

BELOW The first cylinder head is back in place. *(Mark Skinner)*

- The blower is placed on the intake manifold.
- The blower belt is put in place – the valve lash is begun.
- Valve covers are put back on.
- The spark plugs are put back in and the wires put back on.
- Finally, the motor is double-checked throughout.

RIGHT **The blower is placed on the intake manifold.** (Mark Skinner)

BELOW **Finally the motor is double-checked before warm-up.** (Mark Skinner)

LEFT For the warm-up itself, the crew are positioned around the car to watch out for any leaks or other irregularities. *(Gary Cottingham)*

BELOW LEFT The crew chief is in charge of the whole procedure and will know how long he wants to run the motor for, and will check the drive by directing the driver to engage both forward and reverse gears, which will also bed in the clutch. *(Gary Cottingham)*

Once the whole process is complete the motor will be warmed up in the pits prior to being towed down for the next run. This particular moment is a huge crowd favourite. You can see the dedicated fans running between team pit areas trying to get as close as possible to the whole experience. It's fair to say that they don't end up as close to the car after the warm-up experience! For the warm-up itself the crew are positioned around the car, each member knowing what they're looking for in terms of leaks or other irregularities.

The starter motor is connected to the blower drive and spun until there's oil pressure. The car will be run on methanol for a short while, as the timing is checked, before nitro is added to the motor. The crew chief is in charge of the whole procedure and will know how long he wants to run the motor for, as well as checking the drive by directing the driver to engage both forward and reverse gears, as well as bedding in the clutch. He'll also be monitoring engine rpm and fuel flow.

It all sounds pretty ordinary, but when you have a fire-breathing nitro motor sat a few feet away from you, belching out nitro fumes that cloud the pit and emitting a noise like you've never imagined in your life, it's fair to say that it couldn't be further from being ordinary. The nitro fumes are so intense that they form a huge yellow cloud under the awning.

Most teams will fit a large fan to the outside wall of their rig in order to disperse the fumes

LEFT The nitro fumes are so intense that they form a huge yellow cloud under the awning. *(Gary Cottingham)*

as swiftly as possible. The fumes constitute a form of tear gas, and the fans who wanted a front-row view are usually seen running away with tears streaming down their faces and their fingers firmly in their ears. The crew members and driver wear full-face gas masks to filter out the fumes, as well as ear defenders. Fire extinguishers will be on hand, and all doors to trailers and other support vehicles are kept firmly shut to keep out the fumes.

Die-hard fans will come fully prepared with their own masks and ear protection. Their challenge is to stay as close to the pit barrier as possible throughout the whole experience, whilst the unprepared run for cover. In my time with Carter Motorsport this was always one of my favourite moments with guests who were new to the sport. Obviously, we'd try to get them as close to the car as possible, whilst providing them with the required gear. Their first reaction once the car was shut down was always hilarious as they struggled to put into words what they'd just experienced. There were, of course, some who chose to simply run in the opposite direction and get as far away as possible from this massive assault on their senses.

During the warm-up the car will have consumed around three gallons of fuel. The oil is then changed, the clutch is reset and valve clearances are also checked. The car will be refuelled, and then it's ready to head down to the staging lanes.

As mentioned previously, most Top Fuel teams in Europe provide their efforts on a voluntary basis, often using their holiday allocation to make it possible to attend the full European series. This means that for many teams any work required on the cars away from the track must be done on weekends, making their time very limited.

To give a bit more insight into the crew chief's job, I spoke to Ben Allum, who has been a crew member and crew chief for Andy Carter. I asked him about his experience in drag racing to date and what he perceived to be his highlights and best achievements in that time. I was also keen to find out as much as possible about the role of a crew chief in European Top Fuel drag racing from his view:

Ben Allum

I started racing my motorbike at RWYB events previously, but my first Top Fuel experience was with a Top Fuel hydro (the water-based equivalent of a Top Fuel dragster) in the US, with Jim Faulkerson. The 'Nitro Bullet' was a pioneering boat, in that it ran a twin drive system, which is now on all Top Fuel hydros.

In European Top Fuel I worked with Rune Fjeld on Barry Sheavills' car, starting on the bottom end. I've since done every service job on the car from the bottom end to the top end, as well as the clutch. I was appointed crew chief by Andy Carter in 2005 and I'm now designing engine configurations, management

systems, building cars from the chassis up and working as a crew chief.

In terms of my highlights or greatest achievements, two spring to mind. The first has to be my first win as crew chief with Andy Carter in Finland in 2005. We needed something special after a poor showing at the FIA Main Event. We ran low ET, qualified number 1 and went all the way to the final, beating Thomas Nataas and claiming 103 points along the way.

I was asked to put an article together at the time which I believe really helps to illustrate the experience of winning that race:

'Finally the waiting was over, the car was pointing down the track in the start-up area and I got the signal to fire. After a quick glance to the other lane to make sure Rune Fjeld was ready I gave the nod to John Ogden (assistant crew chief) to arm the ignition system. I put a charge of fuel into the blower and gave John the signal to go. He triggered the starter motor and as the motor got to speed I pulled the kill leads and fired the motor. Reassuringly it lit immediately, and seconds later as the nitro came through the motor started to bang out the familiar rhythm you only get from a fuel motor.

'It sounded strong.

'I leaned the motor out ready for the burnout and walked to the front of the car.

'Thomas was moving forward in the other lane so I signalled Andy forward. As he released the brake the car moved forward positively, a good indication that the clutch problem that had hindered us in round two was gone. Andy knew, as I did, that everything was as good as it could be. He gave me a thumbs-up as he approached for the burnout. I could read his mind through the opening in his crash helmet – all I needed to see were those eyes. Totally focused!

'All weekend Alastaro had been a one-lane track. Lane choice was a big advantage which we'd lost with a clutch problem in the second round.

'We were in the left-hand lane. Nobody had won a round of Top Fuel in this lane.

'Andy and I had spoken about running this lane and we knew he would need to be at the top of his game if we were to have a chance.

'Prior to the run I'd walked the track during an oil down and could see that the left lane was starting to come round. There was a chance we could do this!

'I relayed my thoughts to Andy, who was already strapped into the car in the pairing lanes. Confidence was building.

'Andy hit the throttle for the burnout and the car went up on the tyres perfectly. The motor was loaded right through the burnout. It was the best one I've ever seen Andy make. He never let the revs get too high, protecting the motor.

'We backed the car up, exactly centred in the lane, and then it was off with the throttle stop, set the last systems and then I brought Andy to the line. He was so focused on the tree it took a couple of moments for him to respond to my signal that his visor was up. He closed it down and I left him on the blue line. From that moment on it was all over to him. As a crew chief or any crew member, this is the hard bit. You've done everything you can. Now it's all down to someone else. The tension was unbearable.

'The car moved forward into pre-stage, the engine tone dropped as the fuel went on the high side, the car moved into stage and it seemed an eternity before the orange lights came on. The motor roared its battle cry and the light was green. Andy cut a good light and got a significant hole shot, a .060 against a .105. He did an exceptional driving job down a very tricky lane. From the green light Andy was ahead and looked good. The tyres smoked lightly and Andy pedalled a couple of times to keep the car true and then we were there. The win light was up in our lane, and against the odds, in the 'bad' lane, we'd done it.

'I'd made it to about the 60ft mark by the time Andy crossed the line, screaming at him and willing the car down the track.

'The transition from ultra tension to total elation took 5.41 seconds and it is a rush that you just cannot describe.'

My second highlight was the time we raced Tony Schumacher in the US. We'd headed with Andy Carter to race at a couple of NHRA meetings in Pomona and Phoenix, where Andy had hired a car before the FIA season started.

The following are a series of emails that I sent at the time from the Phoenix race, which give an excellent insight into what was going on:

'Date: Fri, 19 Feb 2010 – Pomona was a ****
fest. The car hadn't been touched over the
winter. We slaved like dogs to get it ready, but
just didn't have time to sort all the problems.
We have continued to slave like dogs since!
The shortest day has been 16 hrs. Everyone is
knackered, but we think we are getting on top
of the car. We plan to sit out Q1 tomorrow and
go for a ½ track run in Q2 when it will be cooler
and the track will be better.

'½ track will show us where we are with all
the problems with minimum (yet significant) risk.
If that goes OK we can run 900ft or maybe full
pass Q3. Just brutal! Have worked on the car
solidly. No break, no downtime.

'Fingers crossed for tomorrow.'

'Date: Sat, 20 Feb 2010 – Well ... Another full-
on day here. Although just the 15hrs today so
easy-going in relative terms! We have been
waiting for some head studs to show up to
change the fixing config for the rocker gear.
That didn't show and we had set ourselves a
cut off time of 12 noon to assemble the motor
the old way if the studs weren't there.

'Well 12 came and went so it was into
assembly mode. The blower had been sent to
PSI for re con and came back with a different
front case which made a major job for refitting
the starter cage etc. BTW run time was 16.30.
We got it all together, set the valve lash at the
cold assy figure and then went through all the
mag checks, crank trigger checks and tdc
checks. All OK so into warm up.

'Warm up OK, so into pre-run adjustments.
Running the hot lash No 4 inlet had a massive
clearance. Like 0.300" instead of 0.024"!

'So hot lash was completed, then blower off
to look at the cam follower. Backed out the lash
adjusters and pulled the pushrods. Long story
short, the short block we had been supplied
had the wrong camshaft in!

'The centre journal was 0.100" too wide and
was impinging on No 4 inlet cam follower –
holding it up under certain conditions to give a
false lash reading.

'At this point we had 35 mins to run time.

'We pulled off the rocker gear, fuel pump,
blower idler pulley assy. Removed the motor
snout and pulled out the cam. Had to undo all
the cam gear and refit it to a new camshaft.

Fit and time the cam, set the endfloat which
is 0.001"–0.003", then refit the snout, blower
gear, fuel pump and refit all the valvetrain,
blower back on, set the valve lash at a figure
for cold cam but hot everything else (???????
– anyone like to estimate that one? By the way,
I got it right!). Oh, and we had to pull the mags
out to do the cam replacement! So mags back
in (which needed timing) and just as we were
fitting the starter motor for a 20-second warm
up we heard the other fuel cars going down the
track.

'That is the story of how we didn't make a
pass today.

'Sooooooo now we have a new plan!

'Tomorrow morning I want to pull off the
blower and inlet manifold, release both heads
and re torque them under more controlled
conditions. We will refit the blower after
changing the burst panel and then........ I will be
happy that we are ready to make a run. Q3 is at
13:30 so still a chance even though we have to
run a ½ pass after changing so much with the
mechanicals to check things are OK.

'However... It is forecast to rain tomorrow. If
we don't run 'cos of rain we won't be qualified
for eliminations.

'Welcome to the world of Top Fuel. Please
pray for sunshine tomorrow.'

'Date: Sun, 21 Feb 2010 – Well...... It rained
today, boy did it rain! We did what I wanted
to and lifted the blower and heads as well as
refitting the heads under calmer conditions.
Literally just about to lift the blower on and
the studs I wanted for the valvetrain assy
arrived, so we set the blower aside and had
to pull the heads off to insert the studs. That
done, heads went on again – by the way, just
so you have an idea, there are 5 main head
studs which are pulled to 175 ft lbs, 4 Valley
studs at 65 ft lbs and 8 lower head studs at
130 ft lbs – so pulling and fitting heads ain't
no breeze!

'I decided we needed to change the burst
panel on the blower. Of course that became
a saga of its own with stripped studs in a
magnesium casting – when I say studs we
are talking 3/16" – tiny little baby studs – 40 in
total holding a burst panel measuring 5" x 1¾".
Finally got that resolved. Then got a 15min call

to run. Thrashed but got the car ready and went out. Made the run. It started well – 0.84 second to 60 feet, but 1.2 seconds out the motor just lost all power. It looked like Andy got off the throttle. There were signs of tyre shake and I presumed it was too bad for him to drive through, but when we recovered the car after the run I was amazed when he said he didn't shut off. He said it felt like we had thrown the blower belt, but it was still on.

'Upon investigation I found a problem with the blower drive. We stripped it down to find the driveshaft in the freshly serviced blower, serviced by the manufacturer, had disengaged under acceleration!

'The blower belt had pulled the front pulley forwards and disengaged the drive. Upon further investigation we found this was because a retaining circlip had been left out of the blower drive assy by the manufacturer!

'We have fixed it all now.

'We are qualified – embarrassingly as no 16 in a 16 car field.

'We race Tony Schumacher tomorrow in round 1.

'Schumacher is the current NHRA champion and is the most successful TF driver of modern times with 7 NHRA titles – 6 consecutively. Schumacher laid down a 3.81 today, we have only managed 1.2 seconds of run time. To say this is David and Goliath is to make a huge understatement.

'Still, we are in NHRA eliminations and we will give it our best. We are not planning any heroics. We want to go from A–B and at the least make a race of it.

'Who knows? So bloody tired, can't really think straight.'

BELOW Andy Carter in qualifying for the Phoenix race. He went on to qualify number 16, just inside the 16-car field.
(Ben Allum Collection)

'Date: Mon, 22 Feb 2010 – Well, talk about living the dream!

'Today we raced against the biggest, baddest, fastest, quickest TF team in the world!

'We had 1.2 seconds of data to work from and we had a question mark over the MSD [ignition] system.

'Andy did an amazing driving job. He left the line 0.5 seconds ahead of Schumacher and drove arrow straight. We led beyond half track but Schumacher just had too much horsepower and drove past us.

'We lost by 1.2 tenths of a second with our 3.947 to his 3.824.

'We paired up against the very best in the world. Wc lost No 8 cylinder at 3.2 seconds and we lost by a blink of an eye... Literally.

'It was, without doubt, the greatest drag racing experience of my life.

'It took us two weeks of minimum 16-hour days of relentless work to get this car to this point.

'I/we never compromised. We knew how things had to be and we worked and worked to get it right.

'Today we got our reward. I have never been so happy to lose a race.

'If you want it .... never .... never .... ever .... give up!

'Rock and Roll .... Rock and ******* Roll!'

ABOVE This is what happens when it all goes wrong. Time for a new block...
(Ben Allum Collection)

ABOVE RIGHT ...and pistons! *(Ben Allum Collection)*

BELOW In 2011 Ben returned as crew chief for Andy Carter in what was to be Andy's final year. *(Gary Cottingham)*

As a crew chief in Europe, it's obviously hard, as crews operate on a voluntary basis. This is why three key words are so important when looking at what can be done by the crews away from the track, in between races – preparation preparation preparation... There's such a massive workload to be done away from the track. In the off-season everything is stripped, inspected, serviced and reassembled. Design changes are implemented, regulation upgrades are undertaken, improvements are implemented. System tests are also done in the workshop. There's never enough time.

Another area that suffers in Europe is a lack of testing time. In fact the actual amount of time dedicated to this is very little. It's a combination of poor weather over the winter and limited finance that combine to make testing such a rarity. To be completely honest, most teams do their testing during qualifying!

However, any testing that can be done is crucial and can give you a huge head-start in competition.

During such time, I'm keen to see the proving of any developments. I'll also be looking at the response to changes to engine combinations as well as testing of the management system operation. How the car responds to tuning changes is obviously of great importance, and I'll also be keen to see how any regulation changes may affect the car.

LEFT Testing is very limited in European Top Fuel. Having bought a new car for 2011, Carter, Allum and crew headed for Santa Pod to get some early testing in outside of competition.
(Gary Cottingham)

In terms of setting up the car for a meeting, we'll be looking to do as much as we can and be fully prepared before turning up at an event. To my mind the car should arrive at the track ready to start. However, the tuning is all done at the event, as this is very much dependent upon prevailing weather and track conditions.

There are various ways that we can tune the car, as well as monitoring any changes through driver feedback and data logging. Ballast is one way that we can adjust the set-up of the car, making sure that we work within the minimum weight requirement. If you have a light driver and car you can use ballast to increase the weight to the required minimum without any performance loss relative to competitors who have to be that weight too. You can place the ballast anywhere you choose.

Another means of adjustment is the wing. There's a maximum permitted wing angle of 2°. Within the rules you can have anything you want as long as it's below that value. More wing gives more downforce and therefore better traction, but also creates more drag.

There's then, of course, the engine tuning and set-up. Engine combinations vary and I doubt there are any two the same out there. You have to work within the parameters of the rules, but there are a myriad of base configuration options. Tuning set-up varies wildly between tuners and there are countless ways to set up a car.

As mentioned before, feedback from data logging and the driver are essential when tuning the car. We always use a data logger but have no real-time telemetry. I'll use the logger to download all the data post-run and then analyse the information. I can then make changes for the next run based on what the logger feeds back. A good logger with many channels of information is invaluable on a modern fuel car.

As well as the data logger a weather station is just as important, as weather data is critical. The car consumes so much air at full throttle that the composition of that air and its pressure can be the difference between a good run and total destruction of the motor. We have to constantly adjust the tune-up to compensate for changes in weather. We carry pagers all the way to the start line, which give us weather change updates so we can adjust the car in the pairing lanes to suit the weather changes as they occur.

The relationship between the crew chief and their crew is obviously important, but of course you want a good relationship with your driver too, and good communication can be so beneficial, particularly in terms of run feedback. It's fair to say that some drivers are better than others at this but a good one can provide reliable, quality feedback that becomes an excellent tool for tuning development.

You can of course reference what your driver is saying against the data from the logger – simply put, the logger doesn't lie!

Chapter Six

The driver's view

From the outside, we'll never truly know what it feels like to accelerate from 0–100mph in under a second, or to feel the 6G at the start of a run. I am very grateful to the drivers who in this chapter have done their best to relay their own driving experiences and career highlights in such wonderful detail. These accounts include those from some of the biggest names in Europe, as well as 'Big Daddy' Don Garlits from the USA.

OPPOSITE Shelley Pearson is a graduate of Frank Hawley's Drag Racing School in Gainesville, USA. Many other big names in drag racing have learnt their trade at the school, often starting out in Super Comp Dragsters. Shelley recorded a best in Super Comp of 8.02 at 161mph. *(Dom Romney)*

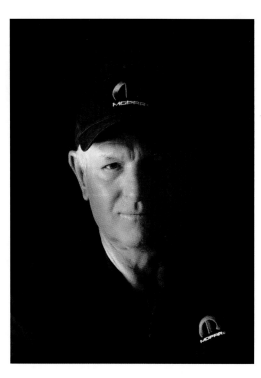

'Big Daddy' Don Garlits

Top Fuel dragster, from the beginning until 2003
Three-time NHRA Top Fuel champion
(The following information was provided by 'Big Daddy' in December 2012.)

Can you recall your first ever drag race?

My first drag race was in September 1949, Florida Avenue, at the Buffalo Avenue stop light going north. GP Robinson pulled up beside me and said, 'Let's race.' 'What do I do?' I asked. GP said, 'When the light turns green go as fast as you can!' GP won, but I remember it well and I was hooked.

What was the first vehicle that you ran over the quarter mile, and do you remember times and speeds?

My 1940 Ford convertible with a 1941 Mercury engine. It turned 19 seconds flat, and when I crossed the finish line the speedometer would read 85mph. There were no top speed clocks yet.

What year did you first race Top Fuel? Can you recall licensing times and speeds?

I ran fuel in my Flathead Ford dragster in 1954. The car would turn 12.01 at 110mph. No licences were required then.

How did you end up in Top Fuel dragster – was it a progression over the years or a swift transition?

I ran alky in the Flathead Ford first, then 25% nitro. I just changed over, as alky was the same class as nitro.

Tell me about your favourite race. There must be so many!

My favourite race was the 1975 NHRA World Finals at Ontario, California. I came into the race over 400 points down. I needed to win the race and set both ends of the Top Fuel record. I did – 250.68mph at 5.63 seconds! The records stood for seven years.

Who was your biggest rival, or who did you most enjoy racing against?

I always enjoyed racing the Greek [Chris Karamesines, an early NHRA pioneer racer]. He was such a gentleman and was very hard to beat. He ran hard, even in match races, but he didn't want to blow up his engine as he wanted to make money, as opposed to some of my other competitors.

I didn't enjoy racing Shirley [Muldowney, three-time NHRA Top Fuel champion] as there was too much friction between us. We weren't friends back then as we are now. She was the most intense racer I've ever known and probably the best female racer of all time. It will take a really tough lady to outdo Shirley's accomplishments.

What's your favourite track to race at and why?

My favourite track is Indianapolis Raceway Park (I don't care what they call it now!), but the best track is Gainesville Raceway.

Can you describe the pressures on the body and what you did physically in terms of training that aided your fitness as a driver?

I never trained to drive Top Fuel as it wasn't so hard on your body, back in the day.

I know it's a big question but can you describe the experience of racing a Top Fuel dragster as best as is possible?

As you stage, everything goes into slow motion. When you step on the pedal you get hit with over 8Gs of acceleration. For the first 300ft it's a little blurry, and then there are the eighth of a mile markers. If you're lined up with the finish-line clocks you keep your foot on the go pedal; if not you abort the run, because you'll be there in one second! You get out the laundry [*ie* open the parachutes] and you get hit with another 6Gs of deceleration! You keep both feet clear of both pedals and brake for the turn-off road, where you're met by the NHRA safety crew and hope all's well. First question out of your mouth is, 'What did I turn?'

Have you experienced major problems on a run, or even a crash? When things do go wrong is there much you can do to correct them, or is it out of your hands?
I blew off part of my right foot at Long Beach, California, and there was nothing I could do about it. When I was nearly burned to death in Chester, South Carolina, in 1959, I had a lot to do. I was briefly unconscious and the car went into a slide. I had to correct for that and then get the car stopped from a 177mph run. We had no chutes then and only drum brakes from a 1949 Oldsmobile.

What would you describe as the most significant innovation during your time as a Top Fuel pilot in terms of both performance and safety?
By far the rear-engine car, for both safety and performance, but for performance alone the Goodyear tyre and the computer. Take away those two things and we'll be running 225mph in a heartbeat.

Who would you describe as the most innovative character in Top Fuel racing over the years?
Dale Armstrong comes to my mind [a Canadian crew chief who was hugely successful in his time with Kenny Bernstein in both Funny Car and Top Fuel]. But innovation is now stifled as the NHRA tries to slow the vehicles down for safety. The Don Schumacher Team is currently the leader in innovation.

Has your own team been responsible for, or is it perhaps in the process of, any innovative design/development/safety aspects that you'd be happy to share?

I used to be but I'm long retired and just restoring cars for the Museum. I like that, as you don't have to blow them up every day!

Back in the day I gave the sport the canopy and the mono-wing. It's up to them to take advantage of these two safety features. There's a little performance to be gained from these innovations, but mostly safety.

Andy Carter

Top Fuel dragster, 1994–2011
Four-time FIA European champion

Can you recall where and when your first ever drag race was?
My first ever drag race was at a RWYB ['Run What You Brung'] event at Santa Pod in 1982. I knew hardly anything about drag racing but had just heard that if you went to Santa Pod and paid 50p you could take your car up the track all day, and this sounded great fun!

What was the first vehicle that you ran over the quarter mile, and do you remember times and speeds?
It was in a just about road-legal, full-race 1,600cc Mini that I'd built for the road. I had it stripped right out to save weight and had fitted a fibreglass bonnet, boot and roof,

ABOVE Seen here in a 'slingshot' dragster, it was Garlits who took the lead in rear-engined dragster design. In 1975 he recorded a stunning 250.68mph at 5.63 seconds. This record stood for seven years. *(Don Ewald)*

LEFT Andy Carter, the 'King of Europe'. Andy is a four-time FIA European champion with a multitude of records and achievements to his name. He retired from Top Fuel in 2011 to concentrate on the racing career of his son Albert. *(Dom Romney)*

Perspex windows etc. I used one of my old Spedeworth hot rod engines – an A-series bored and stroked, full-race cam, inclined valve head, straight-cut box, lsd, split 48 Webers, everything! Anyway, it ran in the high 15s – disappointing, but it had terrible traction. I'd totally neglected the suspension.

BELOW Possibly one of the best pictures ever taken of Andy during his career, seen here in 2010 leaving the line at Santa Pod Raceway. The header flames haven't been enhanced in any way – this is pure power caught on camera. *(Dom Romney)*

What year did you first race Top Fuel? Can you recall your licensing times and speeds?

I did my first licensing passes at the Santa Pod Flame and Thunder event in November 1994. I only got one 60ft pass in before rain called off the meeting.

How did you end up in Top Fuel dragster – was it a progression over years or a swift transition?

I came from Street racing, where I was in the top five for eight years. My first real drag race car was a Ford Pop and I ran in Super Gas for one season in 1990.

What was your best ET and speed?

My best ET is 4.57 at 320mph. This is the track record at Santa Pod and also the fastest time and speed ever in Europe.

Please share stories of your favourite race or races.

I've had so many great experiences over the years and could write a book about them! [We did didn't we? – Dan]

Who was your biggest rival or who did you most enjoy racing against?

I had lots of fierce rivalries in the Street classes and again in Outlaw Anglia. In Top Fuel my first rival was Barry Sheavills – I wouldn't describe it as a friendly one! We're friends now and have the greatest respect for each other's achievements. I did enjoy racing against Kim Reymond and we had some great and very close races.

What's your favourite track to race at and why?

That's a difficult question as I didn't really have a favourite track. They all have their positive aspects, but if I had to choose I'd say Mantorp Park Raceway, Sweden. Not too sure why, but I just felt very comfortable there.

Can you describe the pressures on the body and what you did physically in terms of training that aided your fitness as a driver?

The pressures on the body are big at the start line, and again when you cross the finish line – but only for a very short time, and that's why it's possible without any real problems.

Have you experienced major problems on a run, or even a crash? When things do go wrong is there much you can do to correct them, or is it out of your hands?

I had a big crash in 2003 in Norway when lying second in the FIA championships. I was doing around 280mph at the top end but walked away.

Who would you describe as the most innovative character in Top Fuel racing over the years?

The most innovative character in TF racing is without doubt Don Garlits. I've had lunch with Don on several occasions and spent quite a lot of time with him and his crew chief (TC Tom Lemons, RIP). Don is an amazing man, and comes across as very tough even in old age. I can see why he was formidable in his younger days.

Darryl Bradford

Top Fuel dragster, 2002–05
Currently Santa Pod Raceway commentator

Can you recall where and when your first ever drag race was?

The first race that I can recall was about 1976, when I was four and I ran to the top of the bank at The Pod to see Tony Froome and 'The Sundancer' rear-engine Funny Car backing up from a burnout. From then on it was a case of getting up early out of the tent every morning with my dad to get a place at the front of the grandstands before everyone showed up to watch the racing.

What was the first vehicle that you ran over the quarter mile, and do you remember times and speeds?

The first car I ever tried was Smax Smith's Top Methanol dragster in 1999. At the time renting a ride was virtually unheard of, other than for a select few. That winter Smax had his TMD up for sale *or rent*. I plucked up the courage, called him, and asked if it would be possible to rent the car to get my licence.

My first ever quarter-mile ET was 13 seconds. It was something, but the 60ft was 1.26 seconds, which felt waaaaaay quicker as

ABOVE Darryl
Bradford is
currently the Santa
Pod Raceway
commentator.
Although not a front-
runner in Top Fuel,
Darryl and car owners
John and Lesley
Wright put together a
British team, Wildside
Inc. (Darryl Bradford
Collection)

Truly one of the greatest feelings in the world, and I don't mean just driving the car.

Shut off at 900ft, 5.6 seconds at just under 200mph through the traps, but I couldn't care less about the number. I was officially allowed to race in the fastest and most exciting class/sport in the world.

How did you end up in Top Fuel dragster – was it a progression over years or a swift transition?

I ended up in Top Fuel by default, to be honest. I'd known John Wright for years and he ended up crewing on the Top Methanol car for me. After one very tough race meeting where things weren't going to plan, we had a conversation along the lines of: 'OK, I'll say what we're both thinking. Why don't we run one together?' John looked at me and said: 'You've got a deal,' and we shook hands. I'd previously been offered a chassis from Kim Reymond that was a Top Fuel chassis. We ended up buying this, so Kim's team brought it with them when they came over for the Finals and dropped it off in our workshop. Our plan was to adapt this for Top Methanol, but this would be a huge amount of work. It wasn't until a few months later that I spoke to John, at Christmas, and he told me that for about the same money we could build a Top Fuel car, plus he had the tune-up for it and we'd get paid more at the track to run one. I for one was gobsmacked, but not for a millisecond did I disagree.

On to 2002 and the licensing process began.

What is/was your best ET and speed?

My best ET was unbelievably my first-ever full quarter run in competition. It was a modest 5.30 ET, with the best finish-line speed of 262mph at the Finals the next year.

The last run I ever made in what was the 'Union Jack' car was about the quickest. It was at Avon Park in October 2003, but the clocks malfunctioned and I didn't get a speed or ET, sadly. According to the data it was easily a 5.2 ET, but ifs and maybes don't count, as we all know. I would, however, love the chance to drive and know what a four-second run feels like.

Please share stories of your favourite race or races.

One or two do stick out for me. The first one

it was the first thing I ever launched! The smile I got from that was permanent and the rest followed from there.

What year did you first race Top Fuel? Can you recall licensing times and speeds?

After a season in Top Methanol dragster in 2001, Top Fuel beckoned in 2002. Licensing was fraught – not from a driving standpoint but from a money, team and a getting-it-together angle. As anyone will tell you, building it costs a lot, running it costs more – although when you run it and qualify you get paid, which helps a little towards the cost.

For those who don't know yet, drag racing, especially nitro racing, is 99.99999999% hard work, frustration, being skint, being tired and wanting to quit, but it's the 0.000000001% that goes right that makes it all worthwhile.

There really is something wrong with human nature that you can be *that* down, broke, cheesed off, skint etc, but that minute millisecond that it goes right makes it all worth it, and then some!

My final licensing run was at the end of the session in 2002, after Barry and Andy had just run side-by-side 4s at 300mph. Gulp, follow that!

Big crowd, huge pressure. Green light, right foot planted until far enough down the track so I'd done enough to get my licence and not hurt it at the same time.

LEFT As well as being part of the Santa Pod commentary team, Darryl presents various drag racing TV shows and productions. His best on the track was a 'modest' 5.30 ET, with a best speed of 262mph. *(Darryl Bradford Collection)*

was in 2003 at Avon Park against Suzanne Callin. It was a best-of-three match race and I won the first. The next round on Sunday – well, it was about my worst as a driver.

I'd been paying so much attention to the other lane that my mind wandered and I'd rolled all the way through and pulled a red light on the tree. 1–1.

So the final deciding race...

I'll keep it brief [That'll be a first – Dan], I treed her by over a tenth of a second, ran nine hundredths slower, and, you've guessed it, won on a hole shot by one-hundredth of a second.

The crowd were happy about the side-by-side race, the promoter was happy because it was a good show, and I'd paid my team back in the best way a driver can, by winning it on the line.

However, the best moment came just a couple of months later at the European Finals. We were part of the first qualified eight-car Top Fuel eliminator in Europe for an eternity! We got a first round date with THE man of European TF racing at the time, Kim Reymond.

He was number 1 qualifying 4.64 at 317mph. It was staggering to say the least.

We had a long wait in the fire-up road, and, chatting with him, he told me that whatever I do, don't red-light, because you'll never forgive yourself. He'd done it at Mantorp previously, so I heeded his words. What he didn't tell me to do was not to lean on him and win, so I did

that instead! We got to about 800ft and I could easily see he was out in front. I was on a fairly good run, but obviously not good enough to keep up with Kim. Then the most amazing thing happened. It was like he hit a brick wall and just disappeared out of my view! I went flying past him, and I hoped it was to the finish line first as well. I'd been just about to lift because I knew I couldn't catch him, and all of a sudden I was cruising down the shutdown area saying to myself 'I think I won, I think I won'... It was then that I realised I wasn't slowing down. The chutes were out but I hadn't braked at all, mainly because I think I was in shock! I turned off at the top end to be greeted by Christer Abrahamsson, who was doing TV interviews, and I'll never forget what he said as I climbed out of the car. 'How do you feel, Darryl? You just took out the number 1 qualifier, Kim Reymond.'

Hard to believe it was so long ago because to me the memory is like it was five minutes ago.

Who is/was your biggest rival or who did/do you most enjoy racing against?

I never really had a favourite opponent, mainly again because of not racing so much. The one regret I do have is not getting to race against Barry Sheavills, as we did both run one season at the same time, but never ended up in the other lane, sadly.

What's your favourite track to race at and why?

I only raced at Santa Pod and Avon Park, and I have to say they both felt like home – mainly because I'd grown up at both places over the years, as a kid and a photographer at various times.

Of all the places I didn't get to race, Mantorp Park, Sweden, would have been top of the list of wants, as it always had a special aura about it, from the pits behind the start line to the uphill racetrack and deadly shutdown area.

Can you describe the pressures on the body and what you did physically in terms of training that aided your fitness as a driver?

The pressures on your body are immense. Not a lot of people know I used to be 6ft 5in and now I'm only 5ft 7in!

With a lot of drag racing cars the acceleration is violent. The difference is that in a fuel car, its sustained violence. Once you hit the warp speed pedal it never lets you go. There's not a millisecond when you can move, due to the stages of the clutch coming in down the racetrack. It's like being smacked in the chest by ten boxers all standing in a row, and they've been waiting to take their shot for ages. I used to bike ride a lot and try and keep my weight down. It's not essential, but racetrack days are long, and the biggest risk to driving, I think, is fatigue over the course of the weekend. Add to that, you quite often get bruises on your shoulders from the harnesses when the chutes come out.

Have you experienced major problems on a run, or even a crash? When things do go wrong is there much you can do to correct them, or is it out of your hands?

One very obvious event sticks out. On the Saturday of the European finals in 2002 when Barry Sheavills took his last ride in competitive FIA Top Fuel competition the car broke in two just behind the cockpit going through the finish line. Most importantly Barry was OK, but it can't help but make you think.

Fast forward to the next morning, round one against Micke Kågered and we're the first pair out. I always drove with my hand on the chute release for the last half of the track, just in case. What happened in the next few seconds

made me very glad I did. I was just about to lift anyway, as Micke was nearly over the line, when his rear slick let go at about 300mph and sent the car straight right in front of me and into the field. As I saw it happen I hit the chutes and backed off, crossing the finish line at only about 180mph, to be confronted with parts and pieces of what used to be a Top Fuel dragster all over my lane and everywhere.

Micke's car had disintegrated. The front, with him in it, was in the field, the engine was somewhere else and the rear end, wing and parachutes were right in front of me. The wing bounced by, just, and the rear end was dangling in mid-air held up by the chutes at about my head height. It's amazing what you can decide in about half a second, but I made up my mind that if anything got too close to me I was going to put the car into the field to keep it out of the way.

Micke was OK but we lost the race. I can honestly say that if we'd have been put back in to race in the semis because Micke couldn't make it, I wouldn't have hesitated for a second.

What would you describe as the most significant innovation during your time as a Top Fuel pilot in terms of both performance and safety?

This one is easy: the HANS device. When Micke crashed I went straight out and got one. A lot of drivers didn't like them because getting in and out of the car was harder, but the way I figured it was that it might take a second or two extra to get in or out, but it might save you breaking your neck one day. It was also easier when the chutes came out because your head didn't get thrown forward nearly so far. I must say, after watching Micke's accident up close I'm glad I never got to try mine out!

Who would you describe as the most innovative character in Top Fuel racing over the years?

Globally and in Europe, those pesky Andersen boys – Per and Karsten Andersen, Andersen Racing. They're determined, focused, motivated and clever. Look at how many titles they've won for so many different drivers, and then they went to the States and just about ran with the top dogs on a fraction of the budget.

Kim Reymond

Top Fuel dragster, 2000–03
2002 FIA European champion

Can you recall your first ever drag race? Where and when was it?
I first raced my 1969 Roadrunner 426 HEMI on some track in Jylland in Denmark. I think this must have been in 1984.

What was the first vehicle that you ran over the quarter mile, and do you remember times and speeds?
It was in the same Roadrunner. I think the best ET time was in the mid-12s. The car was completely street legal.

What year did you first race Top Fuel?
I think it was during 2000.

How did you end up in Top Fuel dragster – was it a progression over years or a swift transition?
I started with the Roadrunner, then I raced a Chevy Vega in the CA class. Next for me was a Monza Funny Car, also in CA Class, and a short dragster in competition. After that I was driving a 300in Top

Methanol dragster. After a couple of years my best elapsed time was 5:91, but I had to update almost the whole car, so instead I jumped to Top Fuel. I'm not sure why. I guess it's because it was and is the fastest motorsport in the world!

What was your best ET and speed?
4.64 seconds at 511kph [317.6mph].

ABOVE This picture of Kim Reymond was taken at the Veidec Nitro Festival on 25 July 2003. He'd just run Mantorp Park's first four and 300mph. *(Courtesy Tog, Eurodragster.com)*

LEFT Probably one of the most dramatic photos I've ever seen of a Top Fuel car. Here Kim is storming through the top end on his way to recording a stunning 4.64 ET at 317mph. Everything here is visible – the incredible bend on the front wing with one wheel off the ground, the rear wing bending under all the downforce and the distortion of the rear slicks. Kim's car was tuned by Per and Karsten Andersen. *(Badboys Imagin/Bill Sly)*

Please share stories of your favourite race or races.

I have many nice memories from the track. One, of course, was when we became FIA European Top Fuel champion in 2002. Another was when we were the winners of our first FIA race in Mantorp Park, Sweden. We used four blocks and five cranks to win the race, but we did it!

Who was your biggest rival or who did you most enjoy racing against?

I always liked to race against Barry Sheavills and Andy Carter.

What's your favourite track to race at and why?

I think it must be Santa Pod. It's a fast track and there are always a lot of cars there.

I know it's a big question but can you describe the experience of racing a Top Fuel dragster as best as is possible?

FAST! For me it started when I put on my drivers' clothes in the trailer. I always had a special way and order that I put them on. I also liked to get

in the car in good time to make myself ready for the race. As soon as my team started the engine I was ready for the burnout. Everything else didn't matter, only the car and I. No nerves, nothing else to think about, just to win the race. After the burnout into stage, we took everything nice and easy. Sometimes there was a bit of a staging war where we'd try to play a little with the other competitor's nerves. It was just a game!

The run itself is very unique, because the body makes it feel like most of its functions are useless, other than those used for the run. The focus is only on what is happening, namely that you've just been sent forward by 6G! You can't see in colour, you can't hear, smell, taste, etc. The body uses its resources to handle the speed of time. The 4.5–5 seconds it really takes to run the 402m feels like 15 seconds. Very strange, but a great feeling. Also, it's a great feeling when the chutes come out. Then you know that at least you'll stop again soon!

Can you describe the pressures on the body?

When you run the car down the track, you can always check if it's a good run or not just by trying to move your head forward. If you can move your head forward then the car isn't going fast.

Have you experienced major problems on a run, or even a crash? When things do go wrong is there much you can do to correct them, or is it out of your hands?

I never crashed but have had a fire five or six times, but never anything serious. In a crash I don't think you can do much – just wait until the car stops.

Rico Anthes

Top Fuel dragster, 1992–2002
1997 FIA European champion

Rico, you've been a hugely successful Top Fuel racer for many years. You now have your car exhibited at the Auto & Technik Museum, Sinsheim. How did contact with the museum come about?

In early 1980 there had been some contact between the German Association for Drag Racing and Hermann Layher. They've always

BELOW Rico Anthes is a legend of European Top Fuel drag racing. The drag strip at Hockenheim, Germany, has been named after him and is known as the Rico Anthes Quartermile. *(Colin Donisthorpe)*

been very interested in exceptional vehicles, including drag racing machinery.

Is it true that there was once a drag race on the street outside the museum, organised by them?

During the discussions between Layher and I, the idea developed of having a dragster demonstration race on the road leading to the museum. The spectators at the roadside were very impressed and we agreed then that a dragster display should be set up in the museum.

Drag racing is very much an American sport, so how did you end up driving a dragster?

Drag racing was introduced to Germany by American soldiers at the air base in Erlensee, near Hanau, and it's thought the first drag race was in 1968. On Sunday the runway was converted by the US team to provide a quarter-mile run. Years later I was, by chance, at one of these drag races at the air base with friends, and experienced for the first time the acceleration of a Funny Car live. It impressed me so much that I decided I needed to find the time to learn more about this strange motorsport.

When did you start drag racing?

After my first visit to a dragster race in the spring of 1979. When I found that the racing fever had gripped me, things went pretty fast – like everything in drag racing. It was only a few weeks later that I took with my street legal Golf GTI to a race in Erlensee. I then decided I needed a US muscle car – a 1958 Chevy Bel Air. But this still wasn't fast enough so I decided to head to the homeland of drag racing, the USA, and acquire a proper dragster running in the Comp Altered class. I then spent much of the early 1980s in England and Sweden racing successfully. After that I raced the legendary 'Duck' and then the 'Super Duck' 2CV Citroën before racing Funny Car and jet cars. I finally entered the premier class – Top Fuel – in 1992. [See them all on Rico's website, www.rico-anthes.de.]

Were you previously involved in any other form of motorsport?

I was new to it all in 1979, like an infant. I never imagined that I'd go on to have such a successful motor racing career. In 1997 I found myself in Monaco as FIA European Top Fuel champion, together with all the other FIA world champions including Formula 1. That was for me a really great experience. Even today I'm still the 'Fastest German' on four wheels. This title I took from the legendary Rudolf Caracciola.

What fascinates you about drag racing?

Without a doubt it's the speed and acceleration.

THIS PAGE In the 'Chassis' section of this book you'll read about the introduction of wheelie bars, designed to eliminate a 'blowover'. This sequence of photos taken at Santa Pod Raceway shows Rico suffering a major blowover. He walked away from this frightening-looking crash waving to the crowd, as shown in his portrait photo on page 146. *(Colin Donisthorpe)*

I also like comparing times with the competitors – to see who's the faster. And I like the basics of it as a race – the duel at the Christmas Tree lights, the best response, lightning-fast gear changes and improved acceleration until you reach the end of the quarter mile.

Are you still active as a driver?

No. After the birth of my son, Victor, in 2002 I decided I'd run my last race in Top Fuel dragster for the time being. As with any form of motorsport, there are risks, and these go through your mind as a father. I want to be there for my son as much as possible. That's why I decided to park the dragster in the museum. Maybe it's just a 'baby break' and I'll be back at the drag strip when my son is older.

Do you still own your team?

The team is in temporary retirement at the moment. I've previously hired the car out to other drivers, but it's not the same without the 'steering wheel' in your own hands. [In a dragster it's only two steering handles!]

How does it feel to accelerate to 300mph in under five seconds?

The speed is, of course, breathtaking, and the acceleration of 5G or 6G on launch is like a kick in the back. Accelerating from 0–100mph in less than a second feels as if you've been shot with a catapult! It feels like you step into another world, and the perception of your brain changes seemingly into a different mode. Somehow everything seems to take spookily longer, with seconds seemingly lasting for minutes!

You mention that you've stepped away from the sport because of your son. How dangerous is it to drive a dragster, and how much is there you can do if something happens?

A crash at high speed can, of course, be fatal, but we race under extremely high safety standards, and the dragster cockpit is designed to protect the driver so that hopefully nothing happens. In the US a recent accident at high speed led to a shortened race distance of only 1,000ft in an effort to keep speeds down. I've already had some spectacular rides over the quarter mile. In 1993 my Top Fuel dragster's front end started a vertical climb off the start line, resulting in a blowover. There was nothing I could do except hold on.

You've mentioned your son. If, in later life, he'd also like to drive a dragster, would you say it's too dangerous?

Well, he's started already with a battery-powered 'baby dragster' which my mechanic specifically built for him. Even before school age he showed great interest in the car. It was a lot of fun for him to be at events and help.

We'll have to see about the question of danger in the future, but perhaps the seat in a Top Fuel dragster cockpit is reserved for him.

Shelley Pearson

Top Fuel dragster, 2010 to the present
British female Top Fuel pilot

Can you recall your first ever drag race? Where and when was it?

My first race was at the Easter Thunderball at Santa Pod Raceway in 2011. I'd previously completed show runs against other cars, but these weren't classed as actual racing – although every time you get into the hot seat the adrenaline kicks in and I want to beat the person in the other lane!

What was the first vehicle that you ran over the quarter mile, and do you remember times and speeds?

The first racecar that I drove was one of Frank

BELOW Shelley Pearson announced her Top Fuel arrival with some hugely impressive licensing passes. She recorded an outstanding 278mph with a 4.98 ET.
(Colin Donisthorpe)

Hawley's Super Comp dragsters in Gainesville, USA. This was an amazing experience, being taught how to drive one of these cars and then going to the track to put the knowledge into practice. I remember the first time I released the transbrake the power of the car shocked me, but in a good way, leaving me wanting to get strapped in and go again, and each time faster. The top speed completed that day was 161mph, with an ET of 8.02.

What year did you first race Top Fuel? Can you recall licensing times and speeds?

I got my Top Fuel licence in September 2010. It was a dream, as a young girl, to be a Top Fuel pilot, and at this point it was possible for me to complete my lifelong dream. On my final licensing pass I ran 278mph with a 4.98 ET. This was absolutely incredible, to run a four-second run on my final licensing pass.

How did you end up in Top Fuel dragster?

As a child I was always around drag racing. My father worked on dragsters and Funny Cars for many years, and as a result I was able to go with him. When I'd completed my Super Comp licence I was asked by Top Fuel racer Risto Poutiainen if I was interested in driving the Eagle Racing two-seater dragster. I jumped at the chance! Shortly after, me and my father took a flight to Finland to get fitted for the car and put some test laps down. I drove this car for a couple of years, and some days I could put down 20+ runs, which in the heat was very tiring. Driving this car provided me with plenty of track time and learning curves, which in 2010 made me feel I was ready for a new challenge, that of a Top Fuel dragster.

What's your best ET and speed?

Currently my bests are 4.98 ET at 278mph.

Please share stories of your favourite race or races.

I'd have to say the Main Event and the European Finals, as they're held at my home track, Santa Pod. The atmosphere is fantastic; but the atmosphere at Hockenheim during their night show is fantastic too. In 2012 I was fortunate enough to be part of the night show in Germany and I've never in my life felt on such a high. The atmosphere and the crowd were amazing.

Who is your biggest rival or who do you most enjoy racing against?

I don't think anyone in particular. When you're strapped into the car it doesn't matter who's in the other lane, you want to *beat* them.

What's your favourite track to race at and why?

Santa Pod Raceway is my favourite. It has fantastic facilities to cater for most people's needs. To race at Santa Pod is great for the British fans also, as it's not always possible for people to take time out of work to follow the FIA tour around Europe. Fans are able to come and speak to drivers and cheer us British drivers on.

I know it's a big question, but can you describe the experience of racing a Top Fuel dragster as best as is possible?

Driving these cars takes a lot of concentration, skill and good reflexes. As a driver you need to be focused and also have knowledge on what the car is doing. The car gets towed to the staging lanes, and when we're near ready to run the crew guys will help me get my safety gear on and strap me into the car. At this point I close my eyes and run through what I need to do to be the first driver across the finish line. When it's time to move the car to the start line I'm pumped up and ready to go to work. The crew will bring me into the burnout then back me up ready to race. Creeping the car into stage I've got that bit between my teeth, wanting to win, which means cutting a good light. These cars launch hard and keep pulling and pulling (as long as you're on a good run). After crossing the finish line the parachutes are deployed and then I start to slow the car down. The adrenaline is still pumping a good while after driving. It's very hard to put into words what it feels like, driving a Top Fuel car. My advice? Try it!

Have you experienced any major problems on a run?

Luckily I've not had any major problems whilst driving, but anything could happen! That's where being focused and having good reflexes could help if something went wrong.

Appendices

Top Fuel dragster champions

National Hot Rod Association (NHRA)

(Between 1965–73 the Top Fuel champion was determined by the winner of the World Finals race rather than a season-long championship.)

1965 Maynard Rupp – first Top Fuel champion
1966 Pete Robinson
1967 Bennie Osborn
1968 Bennie Osborn
1969 Steve Carbone
1970 Ronnie Martin
1971 Gerry Glenn
1972 Jim Walther
1973 Jerry Ruth
1974 Gary Beck
1975 Don Garlits
1976 Richard Tharp
1977 Shirley Muldowney
1978 Kelly Brown
1979 Rob Bruins
1980 Shirley Muldowney
1981 Jeb Allen
1982 Shirley Muldowney
1983 Gary Beck
1984 Joe Amato
1985 Don Garlits
1986 Don Garlits
1987 Dick LaHaie
1988 Joe Amato
1989 Gary Ormsby

1990 Joe Amato
1991 Joe Amato
1992 Joe Amato
1993 Eddie Hill
1994 Scott Kalitta
1995 Scott Kalitta
1996 Kenny Bernstein
1997 Gary Scelzi
1998 Gary Scelzi
1999 Tony Schumacher
2000 Gary Scelzi
2001 Kenny Bernstein
2002 Larry Dixon
2003 Larry Dixon
2004 Tony Schumacher
2005 Tony Schumacher
2006 Tony Schumacher
2007 Tony Schumacher
2008 Tony Schumacher
2009 Tony Schumacher
2010 Larry Dixon
2011 Del Worsham
2012 Antron Brown
2013 Shawn Langdon

FIA European Top Fuel Dragster

(FIA European championship was introduced in 1996.)

1996 Jens Nybo
1997 Rico Anthes
1998 Barry Sheavills
1999 Gordie Bonin
2000 Anita Mäkelä
2001 Andy Carter
2002 Kim Reymond
2003 Smax Smith
2004 Andy Carter

2005 Lex Joon
2006 Håkan Nilsson
2007 Urs Erbacher
2008 Andy Carter
2009 Andy Carter
2010 Urs Erbacher
2011 Urs Erbacher
2012 Risto Poutiainen
2013 Thomas Nataas

Glossary of terms

AHRA – American Hot Rod Association.

Alcohol – Methanol when used as a fuel in an engine.

Back-halved – Car on which everything behind the driver's section has been cut away and replaced.

Backing down – Cranking the engine backwards by hand to ensure no unburned fuel remains in any of the combustion chambers.

BDRA – British Drag Racing Association.

Blower – Roots-type supercharger. The blower belt connects the blower to the crankshaft pulley.

Blowover – Term used to describe a dragster's front end lifting so far that the car turns over.

Bunny ears – Popular name for header flames.

Burnout – Spinning the driving wheels before a run to clean and heat the tyres.

Butterfly wheel – Steering wheel designed in the shape of two butterfly wings, used in dragsters and Funny Cars.

Christmas Tree – The traffic lights in front of the competitors on the start line. They're linked with and controlled by the timing computer.

in³ – Cubic inches. A measure of engine capacity. To convert cubic inches to cubic centimetres (cc) multiply by 16.4, *ie* 500in³ is around 8,200cc.

Deep stage – A racer is in deep stage when they roll forward beyond full stage so that their front wheel only interrupts the stage beam and the pre-stage light goes out. The racer is nearer the finish, but dangerously close to a red light.

Dial in – Anticipated ET for a vehicle to cover the distance to the finish line, generally measured to 1/100th of a second.

Diapers – Engine-oil retention devices with non-flammable, oil-absorbent liners.

Diver – Bottom end technician.

Eliminations – Tournament-style competition where two competitors race each other. The winner progresses to the next round, and the loser is eliminated.

ET – Elapsed time. The total time (in seconds) taken to travel from the start line to the finish line.

FC – Funny Car. Fibreglass or carbon fibre-bodied car based on a stock automobile design but with a railed chassis design that puts the engine in front of the driver.

FIA – Fédération Internationale de l'Automobile. Governing body of motorsport worldwide.

Floater – (1) A shaped piece of steel that sits between two clutch plates in a clutch assembly. (2) An extra crew member who assists the technicians in various capacities.

Foul – An infringement of a rule during a run. This may be pulling a red light or crossing a lane boundary line.

Front-engine dragster – A dragster that has its engine mounted in front of the driver.

Front-halved – Car on which everything from the driver's section forward has been cut away and replaced.

HANS – Head and neck support safety device intended to reduce the likelihood of serious injury.

Headers – The eight exhaust manifolds arranged in banks of four on each side of the engine.

Heads up – Non-handicap racing, where both competitors are started together.

Hemi – An engine in which the combustion chamber is hemispherical.

Hole shot – An advantage gained by a quicker-reacting driver who leaves the start line before their opponent.

IHRA – International Hot Rod Association.

In pre-stage – A racer is in pre-stage when his front wheel has interrupted the first light beam just before the start line. Full-stage is only inches ahead.

In stage – A racer is in stage when his front wheels have interrupted both light beams at the start line. (See also *deep stage*.)

Light up – To apply power too abruptly to the tyres and cause them to spin and smoke, instead of gripping the track.

MAG-Magneto – A device used to fire the spark plugs.

MSA – Motorsport Association.

NACA duct – A low-drag inlet originally designed in the US by the National Advisory Committee for Aeronautics (NACA).

NHRA – National Hot Rod Association (USA).

Nitro – Nitromethane. The ultimate drag racing fuel.

Oil down – Situation when a car or bike suffers enough damage to cause an oil leak on the track.

Pairing lane – See *staging lane*.

Pro-stock – Purpose-built racecar based on a production car.

Qualifying – Before eliminations begin, racers must qualify. If a field is too large only the fastest qualifiers will get through to eliminations. Championship points can be earned by qualifying Number One. Typically these fields will be of 8, 16 or 32 cars, depending on the size of the class entry.

Reaction time – The driver's reaction time is the time between the last amber light coming on and his front wheel leaving the stage light.

Rear-engine dragster – A dragster with its engine mounted behind the driver, considered to be much safer than a front-engine rail.

Red light – Foul light on the Christmas Tree, triggered by leaving the line before the green light illuminates.

Roll cage – Metal cage that protects the driver from injury in the case of a rollover.

Rollout – The time between the driver initiating the start movement and the car physically leaving the start-line beam that triggers the timing clocks.

rpm – Revolutions per minute, a measure of engine speed. Often abbreviated to 'revs'.

SAE – Society of Automotive Engineers.

SEMA – Speciality Equipment Market Association.

SFI – SEMA Foundation Inc.

Shutdown area – Area beyond the finish line in which cars slow down after the race.

Slicks – Smooth tyres with no tread. These apply the maximum amount of rubber to the road.

Slingshot – Front-engined dragster.

Staging lane – The designated area for competitors to assemble before they run. Sometimes known as the *pairing lane*, where competitors are paired ready to compete.

Supercharger – A compressor driven from the crankshaft, which raises atmospheric pressure fed into the engine, resulting in added horsepower.

TF – Top Fuel.

Traps – The light beams at the end of the track used to measure speed.

Terminal speed – The speed through the finish line.

UEM – Union of European Motorcycling.

Water box – The puddle behind the start line where drivers wet their tyres for the burnout.

Wheelbase – The distance between the centres of the front and rear wheels.

Wheelie or wheelstand – The lifting of a dragster's front wheels under acceleration.

Wheelie bars – Bars that stick out from the back of a vehicle to prevent excessive front-wheel lift.

Wing – Used on the faster cars for steering control and downforce. The larger wing is used on the rear; a smaller one may be used on the front.

Index